Branding & Marketing for Startups

Startups

The do-it-yourself plan to launch and promote your new small business or personal brand today!

By: David Marcel

David Marcel

Table of Contents

Introduction

About 50% of startup companies in the U.S. *fail* within five years after launch. And over the next ten years, 70% of these companies will fail. Admittedly, I was a part of the share of companies that didn't make it. My startups failed. Twice. So why should you listen to me?

Things in my business didn't really start to click until I started my third company. This one brought in a comfortable salary—which I'm still living off of today. Successful companies four and five followed shortly after. I didn't exactly glide through the wealth-generation process with ease. But I managed to land in the black. And, most importantly, I logged all of my mistakes (and the mistakes of others) along the way.

In retrospect, I've determined that there are three main failures that may hinder the entrepreneur in his climb toward success:

1. Not finding the right audience, niche, or market for his product or service.
2. Not marketing in the right place.
3. And, underestimating the importance of market positioning—versus other characteristics like product aesthetics and price.

What do these failures have in common? The lack of a solid and creative marketing strategy. Anyone can write a great marketing plan, but the creative ideas behind it are what lead to the biggest successes. Good ideas and imaginative attempts ("little bets" as the writer Peter Sims calls them) are the fuel that ignites your biggest gains in the corporate world.

- Anyone can place a bet and invest their money, but that doesn't mean there will be a return.
- Anyone can cook spaghetti noodles, but a spectacular meal will not necessarily result.
- Anyone can put paint to canvas, but that doesn't mean he'll produce a beautiful painting.
- Anyone can jot down a business plan, but that doesn't mean he'll find success.

Impressive success usually only follows once a person has committed himself to a loftier goal. This commitment often comes with great risk—that many people find scary. When I turned 35, I made a promise to myself that I would quit my 9-to-5 routine. I was making a *safe and secure* six figures, had opportunities to keep moving forward, and I was creating solid connections. But, no matter how good things went, one thing was always true: I was always making money for someone else.

Why couldn't I just do that for myself?

Dropshipping was one of my first endeavors. Though I had some success at first, this experiment still brought in less than desirable returns. I found there was too little control over the product for me to feel comfortable with the business model. If a product wasn't high in quality, I didn't want to sell it.

So, for my next venture, I decided to play on my strengths. I had worked in tech for years and had a knack for marketing software. With the rise of SaaS (Software as a Service), I decided to hop on the bandwagon and develop an online video marketing tool. Surprisingly, this venture immediately took off.

The one thing that initially helped us was our effective launch and marketing strategy. Additionally, the product had unique features compared to the competition. However, the competition was fierce and there were plenty of others with strong apps and business models in the space. Still, the quick rise in popularity of our product helped it to quickly rise to a 6-digit endeavor—after only 24 months in business. More success meant even more flexibility with our product, which is exactly what my customers craved. Not only was I giving them something they wanted, but I was able to keep up with the market by introducing innovative features and services that they couldn't find elsewhere.

"Inbound marketing" (drawing in customers via web content and social media) was part of the reason for our initial success. It was particularly helpful in our niche—since corporate types are busy and don't want you to be pushy or sell in obvious ways. These days, even the average consumer is wary of traditional marketing tactics—which trick them into buying something unknowingly. Successful entrepreneurs are too smart to try such techniques. Sure, you could invest thousands of dollars and get triple the return using old, cheap marketing tricks, but that'll last you a year at best—not something you want to do if you're giving a company your all and you want to nurture it from the ground up. Even if you plan to sell in 5, 10, or 15 years, that doesn't mean you're not still putting passion and hard work into it. In fact, you should always be thinking of your business as a machine—one that can function without you (at least for a little while). For an excellent resource on this topic, check out John Warrillow's book "Built to Sell: Creating a Business That Can Thrive Without You."

But back to startup marketing: just understand that a *solid* company is one driven by brand—as manifested via the founder's passion and individuality. In crafting a business, you create a connection between you and your brand, as well as the brand and the customer. Marketing isn't just flashing your product around with a smile. Marketing is everything involved in the selling of a product—from the initial pitch, to the customer's unboxing experience (which is often the most important part).

As Lao Tzu said:

A journey of a thousand miles begins with a single step.

The first step in the birth of your great startup, is the creation of a business plan, buyer persona, marketing strategy, and all the other common organizational aspects that go into running a business.

The next step is brand creation. Marketing is required here because the creator has to consider the color, label, font choice, and everything else for packaging.

Then there is the marketing effort—putting your product in the front window so that potential customers can view it.

Next comes the *customer*. His role is to visit your shop and make a purchase, but marketing doesn't stop there. The product has to work for the customer—ideally, well enough such that he'll tell all of his friends about it.

And, hopefully, these friends will also be converted into customers themselves.

All of these interwoven steps come together to make up the fine art of "marketing." Many of the details in this process are often overlooked—because some can seem like irrelevant aspects of the process:

- The font on the perfume bottle
- The color of the shopping bag
- The "thank you" email—which the customer received after purchase

These might not seem very important. But when attention to each detail is aggregated throughout the campaign (from marketing to product fulfillment), then the resultant buying experience leaves a positive impression on the customer.

Steve Jobs was famous for this attention to detail. When the Apple stores opened, Jobs oversaw every detail—from the type of wood that would be used for the product tables, to the exact angle that the mac laptop screens were to be positioned at each morning upon opening.

Customers have many options these days. They can go anywhere—online or in person. And each place they visit will feature a cornucopia of potential buying options. Some customers take advantage of this—making constant comparisons, trying new things, and reading reviews. Others would rather just make a purchase and go, utilizing "honest indicators" (triggers that indicate a product's probable quality) to make a decision.

So how can you catch both types of customers in the same net? Well, with a marketing strategy that has no "holes" of course. Ideally, we'd like the inquisitive consumer to trust us and to understand that their questions and concerns about our product will be answered, and that their satisfaction is of our utmost concern. But we'd also like our product to be instantly accessible to the customer who just wants the decision process to be lubricated and effortless.

In this book, we'll teach you how to market successfully to multiple types of client personas. We'll be examining three marketing fundamentals:

1. Finding the right marketing channel
2. Crafting a plan for targeting your desired clientele
3. And, creating a strong brand and product marketing strategy

Sound good?

Now, ask yourself, "What are your personal goals?" There are many possible reasons for you to purchase this book.

- Perhaps you have a hobby that you'd like to transform into a business.
- Maybe you're a freelancer looking to expand your clientele.
- Maybe your niche is a lifestyle brand or you provide a specific or regional service of some sort.
- Or, perhaps you're just looking for a home-based business and a way to make some passive income.

Either way, all of us entrepreneurs tend to be in pursuit of the same thing—the manifestation of an idea. The birth of a new business idea is born of our minds and we nurture it—just as we would a child or a garden.

Now, let's lay down the soil for this garden to grow. In

this book, we'll build a foundation of marketing and branding fundamentals—that will help lead you to the success you've been hoping for. It's time to get started with your new startup now!

Ch. 1: Exploring Your Market

There are two important questions that all entrepreneurs must answer before launching a product:

- What am I selling?
- Who am I selling it to?

The answer to these questions helps to determine your market niche. If you're selling baby blankets to new moms, you're in the parenting niche. If you're selling textbooks to college students, you're in the education business. If you're selling marketing software to entrepreneurs, you're in the advertising market.

Suppose someone told you, "I'm going to the market today." You might assume that they mean the local grocery store. Picture this person strolling down the aisles, and perusing the products on offer. This is how you should be perceiving your prospective client. Picture her walking through the corridors of your market (be that in the digital space or in a physical retail shop). Try to see your product as she sees your product. Put yourself in her shoes. Why would your product leap up off the shelf—at least more than the next product? This is where the power of "brand" comes in.

The first step involves getting to know your company. Right now, you have an idea of what it is. You understand the core principles behind it and what you hope to gain. But, you still might just have an idea, and that doesn't always correspond with objective truth.

Imagine you're going on a first date. You meet the person of your dreams and have an instant connection. You go home and wonder, "Is this love?" It's easy to feel euphoric when you only have an *idea* of something grand. When enthusiasm exists behind it, you'll propel that idea into a place of wonder. A casual first date with the *girl-next-door* can turn into the soon-to-be "wedding of a lifetime" if you let those thoughts run for too long. As time goes by, you move on to the second, third, fourth, and twentieth date. Maybe you're eventually living together and more of "who they are" begins to emerge. You never realized the love of your life was the type of person to clip their toenails in the living room or slam cupboards too loudly. Years may go by. You may still be deeply in love with this person, but it's a different type of love.

The point is, your relationship with your brand (as well as your customer's relationship with the brand) will change over time. Right now, it's easy to be filled with enthusiasm. But you have to love your brand so that when you discover the flaws, you're still passionate enough to work through them. This is why it's so important to see meaning and value in the product you're selling. If you don't, then the journey to success could be drudgery.

The core of brand-creation lies in recognizing who you're marketing to. This isn't just a two-party relationship. You can have a strong company, but who is there to consume the product? Your brand depends on *you* to build it, but (ultimately) relies on your customer's to welcome in its existence.

Ask yourself:

- Why do you have this company of yours?
- What are you doing for the consumers?
- Why are they choosing you?
- What do you have to offer that someone else doesn't?
- What will people remember you by?

Knowing your company means knowing every strength and even the most minor of weaknesses. Your story, tone, style, message, and intent are all wrapped up in the development of your branding voice.

The biggest challenges a startup owner can face are *his own assumptions about his company or product*. He may underestimate the competition and initial costs. He may overestimate sales and have lofty expectations for his product's success. Such pride is often the result of a failure to use the resources available to ascertain the product's viability before putting so much trust in it. A lack of research is the shortcut to failure, so equip yourself with an expansive vision of your market before injecting your product into it.

The Product and the Market

Wherever you are right this second, look around. Unless you're in a pure white room, you can probably identify at least three brands in front of you—the logo on the crumpled-up shopping bag in the corner, the sticker on the sliced bread bag, the text on the advertisement mailer…

- Why do you own these things?
- What did you need from these companies?
- What service did they fulfill?

Right now, I see a laptop brand in front of me. I purchased the laptop because I needed a way to take my work outside my home. I purchased this brand because I had used it in the past and always had success with their products.

I see a coffee cup with a logo. I purchased this coffee because it gives me energy and I like the taste. I chose this particular coffee shop because it offers a cozy place to write without distraction.

I see my day planner—where I take notes and create schedules. I remember purchasing this particular brand because it offered the best size and organizational features for my needs.

To get a better sense of *your* buyer's predilections, you have to recognize how your product or service benefits its users. What are you offering that fulfills their needs? I needed a laptop, a quiet place to write, a good cup of coffee, and a customizable day planner. All of these products fulfilled that need for me.

For entrepreneurs, the most difficult questions to ask ourselves is this:

"Why would anyone really choose my brand over another?"

By always striving to see your product from multiple perspectives, you'll be able to modulate your message—to find the correct tone and voice for the prospective buyer. To understand how to best represent who you are to a customer, here are some things to consider.

Taking Your Customer's Needs into Consideration

The reason that *any* market exists at all, is because it fulfills the needs of a customer. People might be frustrated with something that they're not getting from themselves or from another service provider—thus they take it upon themselves to fulfill that need in the market. The importance of breaking down the different *types of needs* for the many types of customers, is an important concept for new startup entrepreneurs to understand. Most importantly, the service that a product provides is "convenience." Products make life simpler (or better) for people. And if the product can make *multiple* aspects of your life simpler, then it's even more valuable. If you need to build a marketable website, then it's easier to have a web development company do that for you, than it is to: hire a freelance IT coder, and hire a content creator, and a social media manager, etc. Having an *all-in-one service* is a more seamless way to make things easier for the consumer. *Convenience* plays a huge role in determining *where* the consumer will spend his money—e.g. where can a given product be purchased easiest? Part of the reason that fast food franchises are so successful is because they often offer drive-throughs. In some franchises, 60% to 90% of transactions are conducted across the drive-through window counter.

Price is also wrapped up in that convenience. Have you ever paid twelve dollars for a stale hot dog at a ballgame? You're not paying for the meat and the bread. You know how to make a hot dog and throw some ketchup on it. But you're paying for the *convenience* of course. This is why product positioning and market availability is so important. Because, many customers will tolerate exorbitantly high prices (and even inferior products), if it means that they can consume the product now.

Note however that these rules are not true for everyone. Some people don't care about price if it means they can get the best quality possible. Others are willing to wait—they might eschew convenience if it means that they can get better service or a better meal later. Consistently striving to understand your primary market demographics is how you can best hope to harmonize the divergent imperatives and predilections of your clientele.

How Do You Stand Out in a Crowd?

What's unique about you? Can you answer this question immediately, or does it take a while to think of a response?

In the world of contemporary commerce, not only must you compete with your proximal competitors (offering goods and services in your city), but you must also compete with companies in the digital domain—the millions of other service providers offering a similar product on Google.

There will never be a shortage of places to go for a specific service or product. However, there can be a shortage of quality and unique businesses—that actually give people what they want *and* make them happy while doing it. You have to discover what makes your company stand out. Why should somebody truly pick *you* instead of approaching somebody else? Often, adding additional features and upsells to a product is often a good place to start.

Maybe you're a freelancer who writes résumés for people. This service is commonly available online, and prospective buyers have many options. However, maybe you could add additional benefits that would make your services stand out from the crowd—like a free cover letter or a series of common interview questions for potential hires.

Often, the service that makes *your* product standout typically doesn't require much additional work on the part of you—the service provider. It might only take you a few minutes to tack on a list of interview questions to your product deliverable. Yet, from the customer's perspective, he sees a company that offers Service A and a company that offers Service A + B. If both services are offered for a similar price, then the latter option is often the more attractive and logical choice for him.

Look at your competitors and see what is keeping them held back. What's the connection that they all have to each other? Can you be that broken link in the chain?

See if you can double up your services. Instead of just offering video content, maybe you can also offer web copy. Don't overdo it to the point where you (or your customer) become overwhelmed, but remember adding services can help increase product appeal and some fraction of buyers will *always* purchase an upsell.

Your Product Message

Your story has a message behind it. There's greater truth and meaning to be shared with your audience. Having a mission statement makes your customers feel more connected to the product you're selling—potentially instilling a sense of fulfillment and an appreciation of value via words. Below we've listed three mission statements. Try to guess where each one came from. (There's a good chance you've heard at least one of these statements before.)

1. "Our mission is to empower every person and organization on the planet to achieve more."
2. "To inspire and nurture the human spirit—one person, one cup, and one neighborhood at a time."
3. "To create a better everyday life for the many people."

Do you have any ideas about where these came from?

- The first one is from Microsoft.
- The second might be a bit more obvious—it's from Starbucks.
- And the third one is curious since it uses an odd phrasing—"for the many people." We're not sure if they chose this sentence structure to stand out, or if it was because, since IKEA is Swedish, they were using a Swedish copywriter who was struggling to write in English. Either way, it's at least a catchy motto.

Hopefully, your message will be inspiring as well. The key here is to keep it simple. Don't write a book or even a paragraph. Your statement should be one sentence and no more than 30 words, but less is still better. This message will help you uphold your foundational values.

- What do *you* hope happens to this company in the future?

- What is it you're setting out to change?

When making decisions and crafting new brand ideas, you can reflect upon this vision statement to ensure that you're keeping up with the idea you set out to build.

Think of The One Who's Shopping

If you were operating a store, you'd want to make sure every customer who walked through the doors left with a smile on their face. Even if they didn't make a purchase, you'd at least want them to be pleased enough to come back a second time. Who do you think is the most loved company in the world? According to an APCO study of 70,000 shoppers, Disney ranked the highest.

- So, what is it that makes them so loveable?
- Why do they appeal to both children and adults?

One aspect of their success is their ability to create mega franchises for children's films. A company that large has a huge buyer persona. The thing is, you don't become a billion-dollar company overnight. It takes decades to grow to that size. Your job is to find the most popular demographic of your audience and then dive into that set further. For example, you might be a more gender-neutral company, appealing to most types of individuals. However, after tracking social media analytics, you discover that you're actually doing best with women in their 30s to 40s. Even if it's just a 30% lead, it's still worth expanding on and creating targeted marketing campaigns toward a single demographic, rather than a broad one.

In a way, our primary goal (as marketers) is to find our "ideal customer." When thinking about your ideal customer, there are a few things to consider. First, above all else, is *age* and *gender*. Of course, on a human level, these things shouldn't matter in terms of judgment or evaluation. But, as a consumer, they can affect different purchasing habits.

- For example, if you're targeting *younger consumers*, then this might entail a lower price range.
- Marketing toward *all female* or *all male* buyers can reveal obvious disparate spending habits based on sex.

- *Income levels* should be tracked when possible. People who don't have a lot of money won't be spending a lot of money. But that doesn't necessarily mean they don't comprise a profitable market, and are worth pursuing. However, if your product is of the more luxurious variety, seeking out a higher-paying clientele may be in your interest.

- *Location* also plays a huge role in setting up your campaign. If your company is a local eatery or a retail shop—physically situated to serve a regional clientele—then this can obviously alter the amount of regional targeting you'll be putting into your marketing efforts.

Fortunately, given the superior analytics and ad-targeting tools that social media platforms (like Facebook) can now afford us, we can target the diverse interests of (not only our current customers) but also our potential ones. For example, if you're marketing a video game, it can also be helpful to know who is interested in *superhero movies*. Marketers call this the "ad crossover." And tapping into such audiences can give you a much wider reach for your campaigns.

Customer Pain Points

In life, we all have pain, discomfort, and basic struggles. Everyone is just doing their best to try to get through the day and navigate the many obstacles of life. Often, the brands we depend on are the ones which (quite literally) can help us through life's struggles.

As a startup entrepreneur, it is your job to recognize the pain point that somebody is coming to you to alleviate. They have an issue, and you have the medicine needed to fix it. To sell your remedy most effectively, you must know *who* you're treating—i.e. who is this person who seeks this cure from you.

The sources of this person's pain are often an artifact of the current failures of the market to cure this pain. So take the time to seek out the most negative comments by your competitor's buyers. Read their bad reviews, and ask yourself:

- What (exactly) is it that your competitors might be failing to provide this person with?
- Where are your competitor's products falling short?

- Why have these customers failed to find an
  adequate solution to their problems?

Everybody knows the saying, "The customer is always right." I personally don't fully believe this to be true. Because, in the end (as entrepreneurs) keeping loyal and dependent employees is just as important as fostering a relationship with our customers. Usually, the owner himself actually does know what is right and what is wrong—after all, it's his company.

However, a customer's perspective is still always valid. That's a subtle but important difference to take note of. The issues that make customers unhappy are problems we should try to work on—especially if the source of their pain is coming from one of our competitors. You might not be able to accommodate their issue immediately. But, striving to satisfy such customers should be a part of your business plan.

Your customers have goals and motivations that propel them toward wanting to make a purchase. We all have goals. For example, you might have the goal of wanting to lose weight. Can you recall the last athletic commercial you saw? It may have been from a company selling expensive gym equipment or sneakers. Was the commercial attempting to motivate you to get fit? A motivational aspect in advertising can help inspire the customer. Good companies recognize that inspiration, motivation, and passion are often more alluring than price. Such emotions are instilled via the successful application of product marketing tactics (and hopefully, via the product itself). People want to feel the way that the people in the commercial feel. They want to "live in a beer commercial" as the saying goes. Teasing at the possibility of inciting such emotions, and playing off the pain points of the customer, helps him to actualize his own position in the development of your brand. Ultimately, it's all about him. So make sure your customer gets all the attention he needs—to overcome the issues he's seeking you out for in the first place.

Collecting Opinions

Interviews are a great way to get to know your clients better. These interviews will involve reaching out to people via social media, conducting in-store interviews, or just logging responses from informal customer interactions. Through these channels, you will get to know the people and what they want on a deeper level. You can better understand the problems and issues that people are trying to resolve with your products. You can get to know them better and learn what is required to help them be more efficient with what they're consuming.

In the online world, a simple method to start with is to use surveys on Facebook or Instagram. You can also have people drop comments and encourage them to respond via email messages from the company list. Such communiqués often have an ancillary benefit—acting to create brand-awareness whilst gathering data.

Ultimately, as marketers, we want to know which campaigns are (and are not) working. Not only does a customer discussion help increase the natural engagement of our business channels, but it also provides us with insight as to where we should be strategizing for our next marketing move.

Our goal is to create customer surveys which ask questions like:

- Where do you work?
- What is your household size?
- What intrigues about a certain product?
- What factor are most influential in determining why you have (or have not) selected our product?

People usually need an incentive to fill out such surveys. Typically, companies will offer a small discount or a free item in exchange for a completed survey. Either way, despite the upfront cost, such data is usually valuable enough to warrant the expense.

Marketing your Brand

Once you're aware of the type of person you'll be marketing to (i.e. once you've sketched out your ideal *buyer persona*), then what's the next step? Typically, it is via the initial data-collection exercise that we come to craft our "brand voice," select the best place to market our product, come up with web content that our customers will enjoy, and cater to more specific client needs. Let's dig a little deeper into each of these methodologies now.

Brand Language and Tone

Picture two different companies: The first is a very luxurious travel agency. The second is a company that manufactures squishy animal toys for children. The language that both companies use is going to be very different.

When creating copy, whether it's a 2,500-word blog post or a social media tweet, the more luxurious brand is going to have very exclusive writing—directed at a certain type of clientele. And the toy company will be angling their content toward a younger audience. Do you see how the brand voice must be very specific for all of your company content?

Picture those two companies once again. Ask yourself, who would you select as a spokesperson for each pitch?

- For the first, you might pick a very distinguished actor with a strong, stern voice.

- For the second, you might pick the latest pop star with a large teen following.

If you tried to swap any of that information for either company, the brand voice wouldn't sound right. This is why you must develop the *language and tone* of your business early. It's not that any given method is better. It's that all voices are unique.

As soon as you hear a voice, you might be able to picture what that person looks like. If you're talking to a loved one on the phone, you can likely imagine their face as their words leave their mouth. It's the same with marketing niches. When somebody examines your marketing material, they should be able to easily recognize the direction that the voicing is trying to take them. Whether it's a Facebook post or an email headline, the customer should know that it's *you* who is talking to *them*. This milieu is created via the words you use, the spokespeople you hire, the tone you set, and your general branding aesthetic. Such branding artifacts should be manifest in every piece of content that your company puts out. So striving for *consistency* and *cohesion* is a good policy when trying to hit the right notes with your brand copy.

Channels for Outreach

There are many different marketing channels by which to reach your buyer. They call them "channels" for a reason. We can think of them like water channels. Conventional channels spread water from one location to another. As startup marketers, we'll be looking for possible channels to spread our product message—from our office, to the advertisement medium, and finally, into the lives of our target clientele. The largest of such channels is *social media*—particularly as hosted via the top five US platforms:

1. Facebook
2. Instagram
3. YouTube
4. Twitter
5. LinkedIn

Billions of users access these sites each day. Within these channels are many possible advertising gateways. You can pay to have posts sponsored or insert ads in between other people's posts. You can reach your followers with sponsored content or you can choose a campaign specifically designed for luring new audience members.

Different social media platforms are better for different reasons. Consider these three types of businesses:

1. A B2B company offering payroll services
2. An organic baby food manufacturer
3. A urban-wear clothing company

All of these could do well across each social media channel. But some will do better than others on the given platform. An organic baby food company might do best with paid Facebook posts—to be inserted in the feeds of parents or young adults. A B2B payroll company might do best if they were to channel their marketing efforts into LinkedIn—where many businesses interact daily. And, the clothing company might do well on Instagram—where fashion and imagery rule the day.

Aside from social media, there are many other channels of course:

- Paid advertisement spots, display ads (banner ads along the top, bottom, and sides of a website), and inserted advertisements (in videos or on other social media feeds) can bring in like-minded customers.
- Email list marketing is a great way to collect and pitch to the most intrigued and willing-to-engage customers—via promotional emails.
- Paid ads on Google searches ensure that your company brand comes up for targeted keyword phrases.
- Corporate or personal websites can lure incoming Google traffic with SEO.

We'll be talking more about these methods throughout the book. For now, just remain cognizant of the fact that there are many possible channels through which to propagate your marketing content.

Creating Content

An estimated 9 out of 10 B2B companies report using an online content marketing strategy—of one form or another. There's no denying that *content creation* is more important now than it ever has been.

For our purposes here, when advertising execs refer to "content" they're referring to anything that can be consumed *visually* and *audibly* by someone else.

- social media posts
- blog posts
- information articles
- videos
- instructional demonstrations

Anything you put on your favorite social media platform or website could be considered *marketing content*. Often, to get started with content-creation efforts, content writers will start by answering questions on their corporate website. For example, if you're a dentist offering cosmetic surgery, you can create an article about tips for a better smile. This would include titillating titles like:

- "10 Reasons to try X treatment for whiter teeth."
- "5 Things to Prepare for Your Trip to the Dentist tomorrow."

On such webpages, visuals always perform better than simple text posts. Nobody likes to read a boring wall of text. So incorporate images and videos in all of your web content. The content you choose should be specifically crafted with your *buyer persona* in mind. And, when voicing your web content, imagine that you're *directly* speaking to the avatar of the consumer you've targeting.

Additionally, it's best if your web content is not exclusively created by you. UGC (user-generated content) can be just as engaging as the articles you post. Ideally, you'll share stories and pictures of actual users using the product. Seeing real people benefiting from the product is often the best *honest indicator* of your product's viability.

For each piece of content we create, we must prominently feature one of our services on the webpage (at least somewhere). Ultimately, our main goal is to lead people (who want to learn more about our product) along the buyer's path—from his first encounter with one of our informational articles, to making a buying decision—on our pitch page itself. Even (in a worst case scenario) where the customer simply clicks away from your website, you've at least created a transient moment of brand awareness. This is why web marketing is so viable and necessary as a business strategy.

Ch. 2: Writing Your Story

For a long while, I thought it was embarrassing to share any information about my past business failures. How could anyone (investors, readers, or clients) trust me if they knew about my weaknesses?

But, the more I dove into my research, the more comfortable I became with failure and with confronting my own personal fears. Most importantly, reading stories about the failures of other inventors (each one possessing a much more impressive mind than my own), led me to the realization that failure is human and common.

It's normal to make mistakes and to admit fault. No matter how intelligent you are or how successful you become, failure will always be a ghost that looms beside you. Even Tesla and SpaceX founder Elon Musk (now the seventh-richest man on the planet) was just days from total failure several times in his career—that is, before he achieved world-renowned success with his ventures. At one point SpaceX only had enough resources for one more rocket test. If this launch would have failed, then SpaceX would have failed—and you would have never even know the name Elon Musk. Thankfully, it was a success.

People like a good story. A good story contains a character—who is built from the ground up and propelled across obstacles and toward success (even whilst acknowledging his flaws). People like to hear about a curious personality—a persona that is the vessel for a meaningful message to deliver to the world. Such personal connections are what pull me closer to the people who inspire me. Sharing the failures of your company may actually open things up for a personal connection that colors the story of our life. These are the types of emotions that you can integrate into your marketing campaigns.

- Think about an innovative technology company that supplies computers and cell phones to millions of people globally—all of which started in a garage.
- Consider a shoe company that donates a pair to a child in need for every pair that you purchase.
- Imagine a reality TV family that grew a fashion and beauty product empire, without any prior business knowledge.

What stands out about these narratives? The value in such tales is easily recognized—providing us with a deeper connection to the product. An "old hat" is just an "old hat" until you realize that it belonged to your great-grandfather. Your customers can always purchase your product someplace else. But, when they buy from you, they become entangled in your story, and you both build upon it together.

When devising the narrative of your brand, here are three important things to consider:

1. What is your story?
2. What does your story represent?
3. What is your brand going to be about?

The key element here is the conveyance of *brand*

consistency. Behind that initial intrigue must also exist a level of familiarity which customers can come back to, again and again—like returning to the warm fire of a familiar hearth. *Returning customers* are often the foundation that supports a business.

So, what's the difference between regular old "marketing" and "establishing a reputation or brand?" Both are needed—due to the ever-changing particulars of the business world. Using old-school tactics (that have worked for us in the past) can be a good way to bootstrap a company. But, recognizing *new* trends and creating a reputation of *promise* and *innovation* is what keeps new customers coming through the door.

Harmonizing our company's ability to sustain such bifurcated needs can be a source of strife for marketers. To understand this pickle, consider stand-up comedy. In reference to the tedium of being a standup comic, the comedian Steve Martin once lamented how difficult it was to please an audience that (simultaneously) "wanted the same thing but also wanted something different." His audience loved his brand of humor. When they went to a show, they wanted to hear *that* brand of humor, but they also *didn't* want to hear the same jokes that they had already heard before. They wanted the same thing, but something different.

In many ways, this is the exact conundrum that we face as marketers. We want to provide the same quality and experience that our brand has come to represent, yet while also taking risks, to provide something new.

Brand Identity

When polled, 7 out of 10 consumers prefer to read content directly from the brand itself, rather than in the form of traditional advertisements or pitch copy. This brings us to the difference between *inbound* and *outbound* marketing.

Recall that:

- Outbound Marketing (interruption marketing) refers to traditional advertising methods in which a consumer (one who is browsing Facebook, checking email, or watching a television show) is *interrupted* so that your paid message can permeate his consciousness.

- Inbound Marketing is a technique for bringing customers to your product pitch page via alluring content—typically on your website, social media channels, or on other platforms.

Sometimes marketing can be obnoxious. We all know the feeling of having to hear the same commercial every day for months at a time. However, marketing is an essential part of brand awareness. It doesn't always have to be a nuisance to the consumer. For example, handing out fliers or playing ads on television can bring in a ton of revenue if done right. But, they're also expensive and potentially cost-prohibitive on a national scale for most new startups. Now, *inbound marketing* lets you create a relationship with the consumer by sparking their interest first and pitching them *second*. Ideally, customers will follow up and seek information about your product themselves—which leads to a more natural connection. In a sentence, inbound marketing is the practice of "letting the *customer* lead the way to a sale."

Personalizing your Identity

If you had to identify yourself using a few different elements, then what would you pick?

- Your clothing?
- The music you listen to?
- The messages you share with others?

We all have unique abilities and characteristics that amalgamate to create the individual we strive to be. Your company needs to express this individuality too. The aesthetics, personality, colors, and overall message are going to help your company launch toward success. Your brand is who your company is. It's a blend of personality, motives, and values. The *brand identity* is how these characteristics are displayed and conveyed.

We all have a brand identity:

- Someone who is religious might dress conservatively or wear a cross.
- Someone who's a punk rock anarchist might wear torn clothes and be covered in tattoos.

Of course, we all know that you can't judge a book by its cover. But, when it comes to your company branding, people will indeed "judge you by your cover." So use this human predilection to your advantage.

As you go about your day, take time to consider the manner and the methodology by which you make judgments.

- What was your emotional state when you reached for that pack of chewing gum?

- What were you thinking when you grabbed that shirt?

- What are the "triggers" that make you "want to know more" about something?

Identifying such triggers, and learning how to naturally manifest them via our brand and product, is the goal of marketing.

Brand Personality

Generally, as marketers we focus on two types of customers:

- The ones you've already satisfied. (I.e. the ones you've already sold something to).
- And, the ones you haven't (the new customers).

When building any new relationship there's a period of time where both parties will try to get to know each other better. This is also (of course) the time in which *personalities* come out.

What message are you trying to convey with your personality?

- Are you looking to fulfill a greater need or is the emphasis more on simplifying a part of the customer's life?
- Are you motivational, inspirational, and deep, or is it more of a fun relationship?

For example, if you're a nonprofit organization looking to tackle criminal justice reform, that's a much more serious tone than a startup focused on, say, short dance videos for teens. The tone and personality (as portrayed via your advertisement media) are both going to be much different in such circumstances. You don't have to always be serious or melancholy just because you're a nonprofit (seeking to save the world). But it's always important to remain cognizant of the emotions you're instilling in your target consumer. There's a fine line between being *personal* and being *too personal.* If you're creating an unrealistic and *difficult-to-digest* persona, then people will be less likely to *buy in.*

Don't focus too much on the "me," and the "I." Instead, tell a story that people can relate to. Personal storytelling is helpful in this way, but unless you (the founder) are actively trying to be the face of the company (and a part of the brand), try not to get too autobiographical (at least not right away). Open up those parts of your personality that allow you to connect with another person; we all have unique things about us and that's what creates such a special person and a brand. But, remember that our goal is to create a brand that *many* people are going to use and identify with globally. So don't let the persona override the utility of your product or service. You don't want to scare them away too early.

Gen-X readers might recall the campaign television spots by Walter Mondale in the 1984 presidential election. Mondale's team put up horrifying video reels of nuclear explosions—threatening instant annihilation if Ronald Reagan won the presidency. Needless to say, Mondale lost.

You don't need to create a *paranoid persona* to get your message across. Fear can be a useful tactic. Somebody who is afraid that "the world is going to end" might be coaxed or tormented into buying products from the person who says that they can halt this impending doom. But, fear can also drive people away and it doesn't tend to create a sustainable clientele.

Instead, try being hopeful with your marketing message. Be excited, optimistic, positive, and inspiring. Whether you have a serious tone or not, there should always be an element of *hope* to it. Even if you are a startup based around something that isn't necessarily uplifting (like a charity for starving children in Sudan), you can still try to convey hope and positivity with your message. Indeed, you may be one of the few glimmers of hope in such trying times.

Make sure your personality is reliable and dependable. Never say that you're about to do something or promise anything without first making sure you've taken the initial steps to make it happen. If you promise a new program or an upcoming change in your company, it should already be in development before you initiate the campaign. Again, your corporate persona should be as transparent as possible. Because, in one way or another, it will be revealed via your marketing media and in everything the company does. Errors and malfeasance at the top of a corporation tend to trickle down—from the CEO taking shortcuts upstairs, to the box-packer taking shortcuts in the warehouse downstairs. Remember, as the founder of the company, it's your job to set the tone that will reverberate throughout the halls of your empire.

Visual Branding Elements

The visual elements you choose for your branding are going to affect how people perceive your brand of course. Luckily, other people before us have done the hard research to figure out the psychology of symbols and colors—which come together to make up a corporate image. The combination of symbology (which ultimately comes to represent your corporate message) will affect how your audience will view your advertising media and, in turn, how much they're willing to pay for your product.

Most consumers are (at least initially) drawn to one product or another by its immediate visual cues. Recall above when we indicated that, in the world of marketing, consumers indeed do "judge a book by its cover." The aesthetics can be the most important part of the purchasing decision.

Visual brand elements can include things like:

- Typography
- Slogan or Motto

- Logo
- And, every other visual element that appears on the medium by which you propagate your message.

When it comes to *logo design*, it's often best to imagine removing any words from the logo itself and then imagine what information you'll be conveying with whatever remains. Usually all that remains is the stylistic elements of the logo itself—the "jewel" as Steve Jobs liked to call it.

Can you conjure up an image in your head of Apple's logo? It's pretty easy for most of us these days. Curiously, the little apple image has a deeper story to it—it references the fruit of the Garden of Eden.

Now think of Nike's swish logo. This one references the wings of the ancient Greek winged goddess "Nike"—who was believed to be the personification of victory. Seems like a fitting symbol right?

Note how both of these logos are able to make a statement without saying a word. Often, the Apple and Nike logos can be found without any surrounding text at all. Readers might recall the days when Tiger Woods was paid twenty-million dollars per year to wear a simple black ball cap while golfing. The hat only featured one stylistic element—the white Nike swish logo. Other than that, there wasn't any other text on the hat at all. Just that simple white "swish" was enough to convey Nike's message.

Now, we note that Nike is a billion-dollar company with decades of advertising. When you're a new startup, it's typically best to give people some explicit information about what you do. So, typography can be important in the early days of your marketing efforts. Don't put your customer in a position where he has to engage in ten minutes of mental gymnastics in an effort to try to understand just what (exactly) you're trying to sell him. Consistency with your message and medium is important—not just for your company name and logo, but also in sustaining the clarity of your pitch.

The Importance of Color

Look around. Is there an easily identifiable color scheme near you?

- Maybe you're reading this book on public transit—where everything is a shade of blue or silver.
- Perhaps you're in a coffee shop filled with earthy and neutral tones.
- Maybe you're in your own home—which contains expertly arranged décor or children's scribbles on your kitchen wallpaper.

Whatever the case may be, the colors of our lives alter our mood and dictate the way we are to feel and perceive the moment we're in.

Notice the connection you feel to the colors around you. Think of the colors that are most commonly featured on the things that you tend to purchase.

- Which colors stand out?
- Which colors tend to appear again and again?
- What does your selection of colors say about you?
- Ever work with someone who wore the same black hoodie every day? What was he like?

- Ever have an employee in your office who wears pink every day? What does her color selection say about her?

Every corporation has a color palette of one form or another. There are many different emotions and moods, which can be associated with a certain color. The creators of the most popular companies didn't just make their decisions based on what they thought was pretty at the moment. These branding decisions were carefully picked and attuned over time.

- Blue is commonly used because it's dependable and trustworthy.
- Green manifests feelings of natural health and peace.
- Red provides a bit of excitement and danger.
- Orange and yellow are warm and friendly.
- Purple and pink are creative and feminine.
- Black and white are always the safest choices.

What kind of color comes to mind when you start thinking of your company? Chances are, you already have a color scheme in mind. Sometimes the most obvious color is the best choice—gardening companies choose green, makeup companies choose pink. Play around with a color wheel and find a shade that suits your brand personality.

Your Unique Selling Proposition (USP)

Your *Unique Selling Proposition* (USP) is reflective of that one singular thing that sets you apart from all the other companies in your market space.

- Why would somebody go to you to solve their problem?
- What can't they get help from someone else?

For new startups, this unique selling proposition is pivotal. Because, (particularly in the tech world) anyone can start a business with a minimal amount of startup capital—so competition can be fierce.

Your USP might be something as basic as an additional service—one that you offer on your website that your competitors don't. Or, it can be something more exclusive—like a certain feature that's only available in your product. We'll be talking more about your USP later in this book.

Finding Your Unique Voice

As an individual, you likely recognize how your personality determines where you fit into a certain place. It can determine who you hang out with, what your profession is, where you live, and what you enjoy doing on weekends. Your brand identity affects your business because it determines where you fit into a certain market. Your positioning in this realm will come to dictate the sort of clientele that is likely (or unlikely) to interact with your storefront or be receptive to your marketing message.

To find your unique voice, there are a few questions to ask yourself:

- Is your brand bold or reserved?
- Peaceful or chaotic?
- Disruptive or practical?
- Soft or rough?
- Rugged or delicate?
- Open or exclusive?
- Innovative or traditional?
- Will you give back to the community or focus on international issues?

- Do you want to grow to reach a wide audience or focus on a smaller regional niche?

Remember, you can execute both strategies simultaneously, some combination is usually best. The manner by which you execute such strategies will dictate the sense of aesthetic style and message that will be most effective with your branding and marketing efforts.

A Basis for Consistency

Imagine some expensive store—say, a jewelry shop or a car lot selling exotic sports cars. Can you envision a specific type of person who shops there? Now consider a specific clothing brand and the type of person who might wear it.

Though not everyone will necessarily identify with every product they buy, it is the case that consistent patterns tend to emerge from the sea of data that represents our buying behavior.

Often, when customers discover a brand, they decide that they like it, and nothing else. This is fairly common.

- If you found the perfect shirt, wouldn't you want to buy more than one?
- If you found the perfect location, wouldn't you want to own a home there?
- If you met the perfect person, wouldn't you want to marry them?

While true perfection isn't realistically achievable in reality, we can at least strive to become the best in our market niche—thus prompting our buyers to choose our products over our (less perfect) competitors. Such positioning will give our business more leverage—enabling us to charge higher prices and offer benefits that manifest a more exclusive or refined buying experience. Not only are such devoted fans buying from us, but they're also buying a part of our brand milieu—which we have carefully worked to foster throughout the business-to-client relationship.

When you can consistently provide top-shelf service and when this consistency becomes a part of your reputation, then this lofty standard will stick to your brand and (most importantly), will stick in the mind of your customers.

Ch. 3: Building Your Marketing Strategy in 8 Easy Steps

One initial mistake I made when I first started my advertising endeavors is that I would use the same initial marketing strategy for every new venture. But this typically doesn't work. Every product is different—usually in ways that we are wholly unaware of. We can't predict why or when any given customer will respond to our pitch. Indeed, such information is not accessible to the customer himself; most people just don't know why exactly they chose to buy something on Tuesday, which they may have rejected on Monday.

Take a moment to reflect upon this. Sure, you like a certain type of spaghetti sauce. But *why* do you like it? In a double-blind test, when presented with multiple different pasta dishes, most people fail to select the dish that features the sauce of their stated preference.

The point is, the networks that come together in our brains to manifest a buying decision, are not only mysterious to marketers, they're also mysterious to consumers. With each new niche, brand, or product, a testing phase is usually needed to determine which marketing strategy will work the best.

My strategy-creation process starts with niche research (and a lot of note-taking along the way). Through the course of this process, a marketing plan springs forth. But there is a method to my madness—marketing isn't something to be entirely made up on the fly. In this chapter, we'll go over some critical steps that will help to guide you through this process.

Step 1: What's our Goal?

As we go through this strategy-creation process, be sure to keep a record (digital or otherwise) of each marketing strategy that you try. This is essential because you'll need to refer back to this log in the future. Often, you'll get an idea one year, and get the same idea fourteen months later. Your brain will insist that this new idea will work this time. But when you refer back to your records, you'll notice that it didn't. (I can't tell you how many times this has happened to me. It's a very humbling experience.)

When it comes to strategy goal-setting, we want to start by setting a benchmark. The first page of your strategy will contain a write-up of a beneficial marketing goal, as well as the amount of *time* that you'll allow yourself to bring this goal to fruition. Specific goals—that have a deadline—allow for the proper tracking of the campaign and they have a tendency to keep you on course.

Remember Parkinson's Law:

"Work expands so as to fill the time available for its completion."

Meaning that, if you give yourself ten days to complete a project, then it will take ten days. If you give yourself ten years to complete the same project, then it might actually take ten years. If your marketing strategy doesn't have an end date, then you may be bleeding money for a very long time.

All marketing goals can be summed up in two ways:

- The first is to make more money. Of course, you want to increase your customer base or increase traffic to your website—resulting in higher sales.
- The second is to simply get your brand out there. This, too should eventually lead to more sales and more money, but it also helps to foster brand awareness.

When you choose a marketing goal, it must *not* be generic. This means you can't choose something like:

"I want to make more money."

Instead, it should be more like:

"I want to increase the number of web subscribers from 100 per day to 175 per day, over the next 2 months."

Notice how our goal has an exact outcome as well as a time constraint—we're giving ourselves two months to increase daily subscribers by 75.

Next, write down three action steps that will help you to achieve this goal. For example:

1. Offer a $1,000 package giveaway to lure in new customers.
2. Start a PPC advertising campaign on Google to test the waters and see what the cost is for each new subscriber—who clicks over from a Google Ad.
3. Partner with a social media influencer to get the word out and lure some of their subscriber over to our website.

Being specific about your goal, your final goal date, and the methods by which you will obtain this goal, are pivotal metrics for marketing success.

Step 2: Finding the Best Channel

When diving into new marketing channels, choose ones that are specific for your brand. Generally, in the digital domain, Instagram is better for younger audiences,

LinkedIn for B2B sales, and Facebook for most general audiences. But the right channel for your business will only be revealed via your in-house market research.

- Where is your target audience most active?
- What are they most interested in seeing—in terms of message content?
- What do they really want out of life?

But don't be afraid to leave the social media world. Other than social media apps, think of additional websites, retail stores, publications, and other ad spots where you'd be exposing your product or service to a receptive clientele. We'll be talking more about conventional advertising channels in future chapters.

Step 3: Competition Analysis

Competition metrics play an important role in determining the scope of your marketing strategy. How are you going to stand out against the sea of other providers and ensure that your company is not going to be trounced on by the competition?

First, we don't necessarily have to always think of our competitors as the enemy. Use their strengths to determine where your own weaknesses lie. Sometimes you have to just let them excel in one area while you circumvent the niche and offer something of greater value elsewhere. Focus on smaller elements and little features that seem to draw people in, rather than trying to net the entire audience. This mindset is particularly essential for new startups—who simply don't have the resources to conquer the world in the first year of business.

One of the quickest shorthand methods for competition analysis is to use the SWOT method. Pull out a piece of paper and write down the top five competitors in your niche. Then, for each of these companies, note how they compete in four areas:

- **S**trengths
- **W**eaknesses
- **O**pportunities
- **T**hreats

In completing this exercise, you may be surprised how differently the field looks, once you've analytically accessed each of your competitors.

Step 4: Market Research

Market research encapsulates all of the data-acquiring actions that you'll be taking to yield further insight into the marketability of your product and the disposition of your consumer. The further along you go with your new company, the more you'll discover about your niche.

It's usually best to keep things simple at first:

- Who are your competitors?
- How many sales are they bringing in?
- How much money do you have to spend?
- How well can this ad spend potentially benefit you?

The further you get into a campaign, the more data you will acquire. The more you learn, the more you'll realize how much there is to learn about your market space. There will probably never be a day when you have thoroughly mastered any given advertisement space. Indeed, just when you think you have a grip on things, the advertising climate will change, and you'll have to instigate a whole new round of market research. This is the nature of the beast. This is the nature of marketing. It is a constant game of "trial and error." (Mostly error.) But that's ok. The trick is to accept that constant change in the market space is inevitable and that any given campaign will *not* last forever.

Step 5: Crafting Your Web Presence

Your web presence does not only entail your social media accounts. Your corporate website and your ads (as they exist on other websites) are also included in this set. Even ancillary sites like Google Maps and Yelp are pivotal in the branding of your web presence—particularly if you have a local business servicing a regional clientele. Recall in the previous chapter when we cited the importance of *consistency* when it comes to brand. This is especially true for the pieces of media that you can control—like your website and business cards. But it's also true for the media that exists on other platforms—like your ad copy and photos—as they exist on sites like Facebook and Instagram.

As companies grow, they tend to spread out into other platforms and advertising networks. If you continue to grow, you'll eventually need someone to manage these web properties.

- How many content posts are you going publish per week?
- How frequently will they be posted?
- Who will be moderating your comments?
- Who will be making ad creatives?

For new startups, the founder tends to initially start the ball rolling by setting up multiple accounts and trying to do all of these jobs himself. But, as we all know, this level of management becomes unbearable after a short while. As your marketing campaigns grow in size and complexity, other hands will have to be brought on board to help steer the ship.

In advertising, there are many hats to be worn:

- graphic designers
- copywriters
- video creators
- marketing experts
- content creators
- content editors
- social media managers

Of course, you could try wearing all of these hats yourself. (We all do, at least for a little while). But, for now, just be cognizant of the fact that, as your company grows, hiring people to maintain and nurture your corporate web presence will be an eventual high-priority item.

Step 6: Off-Line Marketing

For obvious reasons, new startups have a tendency to focus on marketing in the digital domain. Of course, digital marketing is certainly one of the most important aspects of your campaign. But we'd caution new startups to not overlook the utility of conventional off-line marketing.

Traditional advertising—like billboards, posters, t-shirts, and mailers—still work, and are still used by some of the biggest tech companies in the nation. Have you ever received a mailer from Google? The ones in the white envelopes which contain a little card—diligently promising $100 free advertising dollars for merely using their ad network. (Personally, I've spent over $1000 dollars using these little coupons.) Google sends them out because they work. The reason you go to your mailbox every day and have to shuffle through reams of junk mail (even in our supposedly enlightened age of email) is because junk mail still works.

So, when you're instigating a marketing campaign for your new app or tech product, just remain cognizant of the fact that many fortunes were built using conventional paper adverts and mailers as the primary ad channel.

Step 7: Budget

Your *marketing budget* depicts the amount of money that you're willing to spend to market your product or service. In a sense, your marketing budget is the number of "chips" that you're willing to lose—gambling in the great casino that is the business world. Since none of us can predict the future, we ultimately just don't know which campaigns will succeed and which ones will fail. Remember, most will fail.

Multi-billion dollar corporations (who have been in the marketing space for generations) still lose millions of dollars each year on failed marketing campaigns. No formula will guarantee campaign success. That's why it's so important to select a budget before the campaign process gets too far along.

To get a sense of how much you should be spending, most startups spent around 10% of net profit. This value could increase up to 20%—depending on how established the company is (or becomes). You might initially go up as high as a quarter percent. But, even long-established businesses rarely go down below 8%.

The more room in your budget for marketing, the more eager you might be to spend the cash available. But be cautious of this approach. Ad spending can often seem to function like medication. The first two pain killers you buy may work wonders on your body. But if you put two more in, they may do nothing. Or, you might even get sick.

Successful marketing campaigns seem to function in a similar fashion. They tend to scale up very quickly—becoming more and more profitable as you dump money into them. But, eventually a max peak is met—and increasing your ad spend doesn't seem to result in more sales. At this point, you're just bleeding money.

So, be cognizant of this phenomenon. Sometimes, you can only reach so many people with the same campaign. The best strategies start small and then *gradually* increase until a maximum is reached. Our goal is to find that sweet spot—where we're injecting just the right amount of funds into any given campaign and getting a satisfactory return on our investment.

Step 8: Use KPIs to Track Progress

KPIs are your *Key Performance Indicators*. They are the metrics that every company must track and manage in order to objectively quantify their successes and failures. It is typical for new business owners to only select one KPI:

"How much money am I making?"

And, when we're all first starting out in business, this is often the only number we really care about. But eventually, you'll have to develop a more nuanced view of your company—particularly as you are tracking the performance of advertising campaigns.

For each new campaign that you start, consider what your primary KPIs could be. What are the metrics in any given project you start, such that, if these metrics were to go up, the net result would be (in some way) beneficial to your company?

For example, doubling the size of your corporate customer email list on Monday, might not make you any more money on Tuesday. So if your only KPI was, "how much money am I making" then this increase would have no value to you. But of course, we all know that doubling the size of a customer list would have obvious value to any company. This is why it's so important to try to quantify multiple aspects of your business (other than money) which may eventually lead to increased sales.

Web-based companies often track things like:

- The average time a user spent on a website.
- The amount of time a user spent watching videos.
- The number of ads a user saw.
- The number of products in the user's shopping cart.
- How far along the user got in his web signup form.
- The number of times a user returns to the website per week.

- The number of users who picked up the phone to call the website phone number.

Such KPI metrics might not immediately lead to increased revenue. But they are important because companies know that increasing user engagement and monitoring the effectiveness of ancillary ad campaign metrics will eventually lead to business success.

Ch. 4: Copywriting Essentials for Startup Marketing

What is Copywriting

If you're going to learn how to do *marketing for your startup*, then you'll first have to learn about how to read a *marketing message*. The set of typographical characters (that comprise the text of any advertisement campaign) is called the "copy." Befittingly, a "copywriter" is a person whose job it is to write such messages. If you've ever signed up to a website, downloaded an app, or bought oven mitts on Amazon.com, then you've been subject to the enchantments of a professional copywriter.

This does not imply that, as a startup owner, you should necessarily *also* be a copywriter. On the contrary, you should plan on delegating such tasks when possible. However, when we all start out in business, all of us entrepreneurs write our own ads (at least for a little while). And all business owners are (ultimately) responsible for molding our brand message to fit our own desires and beliefs about the course of the company. So, even if you don't plan on being a full-time copywriter, it's at least beneficial for you to have cursory knowledge about how copywriters think and about which advertising techniques tend to work well on people. We've set up this chapter as a "copywriting crash course"—designed to give you a shove in the right direction with your marketing efforts.

What makes a copywriter "good"

The goal of a copywriter is to create marketing material with a persuasive message—one that prompts the target consumer to take action. This action might entail buying a product, visiting a website, clicking a link, downloading an infographic, signing up to an email list, making a phone call, etc....

Good copywriters know how to get the attention of an audience. They know how to produce a creative marketing message—specifically designed to lure readers and encourage product sales. To put it simply, a copywriter's job is to "turn words into cash."

As a business owner, you don't necessarily have to be a good copywriter yourself. However, you should be able to recognize one when you meet one. This isn't as difficult to do as it might seem. Because, when it comes to other forms of human creative effort (like writing fantasy novels or film scripts) then the quality of the writing is often highly subjective. Who is to really say if one book is better than another? However, when it comes to copywriting, we actually have a much more objective metric with which to judge the piece. Remember, in copywriting, our only goal is to "turn words into cash." So "good copywriting" is that which succeeds in doing just *that*. Good copywriting converts customers into buyers.

If marketing *Campaign A* contains copy which resulted in fifty new buyers, and *Campaign B* had all the same characteristics save for a different piece of copy that only resulted in three buyers, then *Campaign A* had "better copywriting" than *Campaign B*. Do you see why tracking ad metrics is so important in this industry? Ultimately, you know you've written *good copy*, when the resultant stats are favorable—indicative of a target clientele that has been incited to hand over their hard-earned cash for your product or service.

The Parts of the Copywriter's Message

In general, you can break the copywriter's message down into just three parts: the *headline*, the *copy*, and the *call-to-action*.

- **The Headline** is that bold blurb of text that lies along the top of any piece of advertising media. It's the initial burst of text that grabs the viewer's attention.

- **The Copy**, refers to all the words below the headline—which typically comprise the majority of your advertising message.
- **The Call-to-Action** is the final advertising element, which prompts the user to perform an action. In traditional copywriting, the call-to-action might request that the reader "call this phone number" or "inquire today!" On web documents, however, this call-to-action is often paired with an "Add to Cart" button—that moves the reader on to the checkout screen.

A good copywriter knows how to synergize each of these component parts—creating a piece of advertising media that drives readers and viewers toward the ultimate goal of getting them to buy something. Let's briefly discuss each of these three components now.

Component 1: The Headline

Whether you're looking at a magazine, a newspaper, a television commercial, or a website, the first blurb of content you see can be considered the "headline" of this advertisement media. Traditionally, it boasts the biggest type font on the page. Which is fitting since the job of the headline is to lure you in—by any means necessary.

For any given piece of content that comes across your field of view, it is estimated that 80% of readers will (at least) read the content headline. Indeed, that is often the *only* thing they read on that page. If you stop to think about it, this makes sense. Consider how many webpages, videos, and commercials are pining for your attention—during every waking minute you spend staring at a web browser (on your phone or at the PC). These flashes of information only have a fraction of a second to get you to pay attention to them. So they use short titillating headlines to make this happen. Note the emotions you feel when you're standing in line at the checkout counter in your local grocery store. Note the flurry of tabloid text that buzzes around you. How are these headlines affecting your mental state? Each one was crafted in such a way that it appeared to demand your immediate attention, to create a sense of fascination or anticipation.

The "4-U Formula" for Headline Creation

Volumes of information and research experiments exist to teach copywriters what to look for in a headline. But for our purposes here, we can get pretty far just by employing the famous "4-U Formula." When composing your headline, try to make it: *Useful*, *Unique*, *Ultra-specific*, and *Urgent*.

Let's go over each of these points now.

1. **Useful**. Think about the content that came across your eyeballs today—while scrolling through Instagram, watching TV, or looking at a magazine. Which bit of content grabbed your attention? Which bit caught your eye? To find your audience, understand what is most useful to them. Understand what they are looking for. Ultimately, people will only respond to your message if it has a satisfactory response to the consumer's most important question: "What's in it for me?"

2. **Unique**. Your headline should be "unique" in that it is crucial that it "stands out in a crowd." Obviously, consumers are pelted with competing marketing headlines throughout their lives. In our media-saturated environment, we encounter such messaging from the moment we get up, to the moment we go to bed. So, when you're considering the headline of your marketing message, ask yourself if it is really much different than the message of your competitor.

3. **Ultra-specific**. The more specific your headline is, the more valuable it will be. Highly specific headlines often work well (particularly in the online space) because the audience knows exactly what they're getting into before they click. Here are some examples of specific headlines:

    -   The 3 warm up exercises you should always do before each training session.
    -   5 new software tools for professional graphic designers.
    -   The 10-step guide for establishing yourself as a food critic.

4. **Urgent**. Smart copywriters try to add an element of urgency to their headlines—in an effort to compel the reader into performing a specific action *now* (rather than later). The urgency factor can be useful because it forces the reader to consider our pitch immediately—in the moment—rather than "thinking about it" and considering the pitch "later" (which usually means "not at all"). Among the *Four U's*, this last one *"urgency"* is often the trickiest to insert into headlines. Here are some phrases that can help convey this emotion: "act now," "call today," "get satisfaction instantly," "get instant relief," "time is running out", "stores will be closing soon." Using words like this adds a sense of hurriedness to the text.

Remember, the purpose of the 4-U Formula is to provide your audience with a *useful, unique, urgent,* and *ultra-specific* solution to their problems. Such headlines solve the reader's problem and (hopefully) succeed in converting browsers into buyers.

Rapid Headline-Generation Techniques

To get the gears of your brain spinning, I'll list three of my favorite headline-creation shortcuts here.

Try Doing a Brain-Dump

In this method, we sit down and generate as many appealing headlines as we can, as fast as we can. Via a "stream of consciousness" style data dump, you'll probably end up with a couple of good headlines (and a lot of bad ones too). But that's ok. The point is not to dwell on the process or think too hard about the creation of each headline. Instead, we just want to get pen to paper and brainstorm through some ideas. Don't make it difficult. Just make it a goal to get five to ten headlines down on paper, as fast as possible. And then, sit back and choose the most appealing headline of the batch. Then ask yourself, how could I make this one headline better?

Look at product reviews from Amazon users

In this method, we can utilize Amazon to create great headlines for us. If you're selling a physical product similar to an existing product on Amazon or eBay, then find the pages of these competing products and read the reviews. You'll notice that reviews on Amazon can receive "upvotes" and "downvotes." So, look for the up-voted reviews and borrow ideas for your headlines here.

An example of an Amazon review might be:

I've read a lot of stuff about freelance writing, but this book answered my questions. It provided a complete step-by-step system and it's the only guide I actually use.

This is a nice Amazon review. And, we can derive some juicy headlines from this quote, such as:

- Follow this e-book's step-by-step guide to land your first freelancing gig.
- We've got the only freelancing guide that you'll actually use!
- A complete system—to start your freelance writing career the right way.

Notice how our three headlines are using language that was derived from the original reviewer's observations. By composing our headlines based on benefits that an actual customer actually cited, we typically have a better shot of creating headline copy that will be appealing to our customer base.

See which websites are ranking on Google

A third shortcut to come up with great headlines is to simply analyze the headlines of the top 10 results on Google. Remember, Google's job is to display the search results that people want. If nobody clicks on these search results, then Google knows that the webpage was not what most people were looking for. Thus, you can think of Google as a "big contest"— where the best headline wins (gets the most clicks).

Other factors go into Google ranking of course. So you don't necessarily always want to simply craft your headline based on the first search result of course. But get in the habit of (at least) reading the headlines of the top 3 or 4 websites in your product niche. Note the language they're using. You want to become intimately familiar with how these websites appeal to their customers, and how they effectively utilize the jargon of their industry to attract clicks.

Component 2: The Copy

Writing *ad copy* is much different than writing the *ad headline*. Remember, with the headline, we're trying to lure the reader in. We're trying to interrupt the reader during his daily affairs and get him to acknowledge our presence—to take a moment to see how our product can make his life better. But once our reader has passed the ad headline, he'll be reading our "ad copy"—the larger body of text (under the headline), that contains the bulk of our product message.

The exact nature of your ad copy will be entirely dependent upon your *product niche* as well as the *marketing channel* on which this copy will appear. There are also some very important size constraints when it comes to choosing copy length. For example, if your ad is appearing in a magazine, then your ad copy may consist of several hundred words. But, if your ad copy merely appears below a web link (say, for a Google AdWords PPC campaign), then your ad copy might only comprise one or two sentences.

In either case, there are some general principles that apply to *ad copy*-creation—regardless of the size of the publication. We'll go over four key rules now.

Rule 1: Know your audience

To write compelling copy you must first thoroughly understand the audience that you're trying to reach? So make sure you can answer the following questions:

- "Who are you writing for?"
- "What does your audience need?"
- "What does your audience respond to?"

Always striving to develop an awareness of your target demographic is the key to generating "good copy"— which they'll be receptive to. If you know them well, then you'll know what tends to inspire them to action. To get in the right headspace, start by developing a "buyer persona" for your client. A "buyer persona" is a prototypical representation of your target customer—usually conceived using consumer studies, demographic research, or market experience. To create one, you might first start by considering the questions that this person might be pondering—questions that reveal her background and mode of living.

- What is her daily routine?
- What is her job?
- What ideas and goals does she have?
- What challenges is she facing?
- What are her shopping preferences?

Knowing these items about your target demographic will reveal valuable insight—that should help you to generate more effective copy.

Rule 2: Know the difference between "Features" and "Benefits"

Before sitting down to write about your product there are some product-specific questions that you should be prepared to answer. Ask yourself:

1. What are the benefits that my product offers, compared to others in my niche?
2. What words will I be using to grab my reader's attention and callout the unique aspects of my product?
3. What will cause my copy to "stand out" from the competing ads?
4. How will I know if I am succeeding in convincing my reader? What metric will I be tracking?

As the startup founder, you should be intimately familiar with the *actual* value that your product has to offer to your consumers. You should be able to describe your product's benefits using clear (simple to understand) terms—and in such a way that your viewer is convinced that no other product is capable of providing the same service that yours is. The more benefits your product has, the more value it will provide to the consumer. But often copywriters make the mistake of confusing *benefits* and *features*; there is a vast difference between these two.

Features of a product are like the features of your face, such as your eyes, nose, and ears. But these features have benefits. For instance, the eyes allow you to see colors. The nose is for smelling. And your mouth is for tasting.

Simply put:

- The **features** are the "product characteristics" that are designed into the product—utilized to perform a function.
- And, the **benefits** of the product, are the value you garner from those functions.

A feature of your iPhone may be that it can store 10 gigabytes of music on its internal drive. But the *benefit* is that you have instant access to your own personal library of music—all in one pocket-sized white box.

Rule 3. Tell a story with your copy

Some of the best advertisements have the ability to grab their viewers' attention and persuade them into making a purchase via excellent storytelling. Storytelling is a powerful tool in marketing because humans are naturally designed to attend to enthralling stories— especially ones that incite emotion. Invoking this phenomenon in your online ad copy is a powerful way to make your target prospect associate positive feelings with your product. If you can hit the bullseye with your ad copy—activating all of your client's senses and succeeding in adequately describing how he or she will feel when your product is in his possession—then a sale is almost guaranteed.

Two elements often play the largest role in boosting the effectiveness of your ad copy—logic and emotion. There's a reason why good commercials (and powerful marketing presentations) often make you laugh or cry. These displays create emotional moments which make people continue to read the ad. So, hopefully *your* copy will leave a mark on your audience's heart and mind too. Particularly, if your aim is to convert your marketing prospects into a *long-lasting* client.

Rule 4: Use Social Proof

People usually need a reason to listen to your message. To accomplish this, copywriters often appeal to authority, appeal to research data, or rely on celebrity endorsements. As you're writing your copy, put yourself in the reader's shoes and keep asking yourself:

- Why should people listen to what I'm saying?
- Why should they listen to me?
- Why should people take my suggestion?

Suppose you're browsing for products online, and you come across two competing products.

- One product has thousands of positive reviews (from admiring fans).
- And the other product just launched yesterday (and has no reviews).

Or, suppose that you learn that one tennis racket is used by Serena Williams. And another contains a name brand that you don't' recognize.

- Which racket do you think is better?
- Which product do you think will get more sales today?

As we're all aware, the product with the most reviews usually wins. And, the product with the most social proof (celebrity endorsements or otherwise) usually sells better. The brain has a natural preference—to follow the behavior of the crowd in most circumstances. Website reviews, ratings, and endorsements from authority figures are the ultimate form of online "social proof." Social proof is often considered the most powerful motivator in the buying decision. And, for new products, it can be the most difficult signal to obtain. When it comes to writing copy, typical forms of social proof include:

- Customer testimonials
- Case studies
- Starred ratings
- Certification badges
- Editor's Choice Awards
- Endorsement by doctors and medical professionals
- Endorsement by industry leaders

Facts and visual statistics can make copy compelling too. Stating credible research data (particularly about interesting findings) is a good way to gain consumer confidence—especially when the citation comes from an industry leader or a recognizable face.

Always remember, people are busy. They don't have the time or the will to research every question in life before arriving at a solution. If we all did that, it would take us a decade of study each time we decided to buy a new pair of shoes. Obviously, our lives are too short for that. That's why social proof has so much utility to both consumers and marketers. People don't pay attention to copy that's not appealing or useful. Ultimately, it is the value you offer, that determines the success of your ad. Avoid ethereal commentary or nonsensical banter. Instead, work hard to succinctly and clearly transpose the "value of your product" into clear and compelling words.

Component 3: The Call-to-Action

After Component 1 ("the headline") and Component 2 ("the copy"), we have arrived at the final component of our marketing pitch—the "call-to-action." The call-to-action is the piece of content at the end of your marketing message, which tells the reader (or viewer or listener) what you want him to do next. For example:

"If you're ready to own the best-smelling cat litter on the market, then click the Add-to-Cart button now!"

Notice how this sentence tells the web visitor exactly what he is getting (he's buying new kitty litter), and exactly what to do next to get it (click the Add-to-Cart button now). As with everything else in copywriting, the nature of the call-to-action will be dependent upon the medium that you're publishing in.

- If your ad is broadcasted over radio, then the call-to-action might be a phone number that you'd like the listener to call.
- If you're writing an email, then the call-to-action is usually a link—which you'd like the reader to follow to your website.
- If your ad copy is on a website product page, then your call-to-action is often in the form of an Add-to-Cart button—which leads the user through a checkout process.

No matter the medium that hosts the ad, the underlying principles of the call-to-action are the same. It's the last step in our ad message—where we ask our audience to make a decision regarding our offer. If you have been successful in keeping your target interested in your product thus far (with your headline and your ad copy), then the call-to-action is where he decides to "pull the trigger."

The notion that your ad should contain a call-to-action might sound obvious to you. But you might be surprised to learn that neglecting to place a call-to-action on an advertisement is the most common marketing mistake.

- Consider the number of times in your life that you've found yourself on a website, only to reach the bottom of the page having absolutely no idea about what the product is nor what the website expects you to do next.
- How many times have you flipped through a brochure looking for the contact information of the company, only to failed to locate it without a rigorous search, and sometimes not at all.

Clarity and brevity are of the utmost importance when crafting a call-to-action. Your call-to-action is your chance to clearly and explicitly tell your audience what to do next. And, what they will get—if they follow your instructions. Again, recall that the customer's mind is always trying to answer the question, "What's in it for me?"

It's ok to be creative, but be straightforward and clear. Use few words (only the most essential ones), scrutinize over your word-choice, make every word count, and (most importantly) tell the user what you want him to do next.

When it comes to online marketing, always be cognizant of the fact that the internet is a complicated place. When you present people with too many choices, it's easy for them to become anxious, annoyed, and confused. On any given advert, you may have multiple ways to convert a reader into a customer (of some sort).

- You may sell multiple physical products.
- You may have ten social media share buttons.

- You may have multiple email boxes—whizzing around the user's screen—each one prompting him to sign-up for some free bonus offer.

On the Internet, information overload is easy to incite. Too much data will scare your customer away. So, when you're crafting your call-to-action, try to limit the user's choices down to one or two options. You may want him to:

- Call this phone number.
- Click this link to learn more.
- Click here to download our app.
- Click "Add to Cart" to get the product today.

These are typical. But don't make the mistake of offering anything much more exotic. Remember, people gravitate toward the familiar. Your call-to-action must feel as commonplace and casual as possible. If the viewer in some way feels insecure or unsure about how or what he's about to buy, then he is less likely to buy it.

Keep a Swipe File with your Campaign Metrics

Now that you understand the three essential components of the copywriter's message, you can use this information to better evaluate the marketability of your ad copy. Or, (if you're so brave) to compose your own marketing ads. Either way (and as we've tried to diligently emphasize in previous chapters), it's very important to keep a detailed log of each marketing campaign. This entails saving product photographs, storing performance indicators, relevant ad metrics, and saving the text of each ad. This is important because composing a new campaign on a blank white piece of paper can be a daunting task. Trust me, this job is made 100-times easier if you have an existing body of campaign knowledge to pull from. This repository acts as a valuable store of data—indicating what has (and has not) worked for you in the past.

Copywriters sometimes call such a document a "swipe file." A swipe file is a collection of ad copy (the headline, the article copy, and the call-to-action) that contains already-proven textual templates for your company's marketing efforts. When a copywriter needs inspiration, or when he gets *stuck* trying to produce a unique ad, he can refer to the swipe file to start generating and seeding new ideas based on previous ones.

Additionally, not only should you be keeping a swipe file for your company, but one for your competitors as well. The same copy that works in one business can often apply to another. To get you started try visiting the (very useful) website SwipeFile.com to see a bottomless list of popular ad snippets.

As a startup entrepreneur, you should make it part of your job to thoroughly maintain a library of marketing examples—both the ones that worked for you, the ones that didn't work for you, and the ones you'd like to try out someday. Moreover, you should review these files repeatedly so that they leave an impression in your mind—reminding you of which ad characteristics your consumers actually respond to (and which ones they didn't respond to). This is essential because, as product creators, we are often so easily blinded to the way that our target consumer will perceive our product. By maintaining a swipe file (and the metrics associated with the success of each ad), we can train our brain to overcome such biases—forcing us to see our company (not through our own eyes), but through the eyes of a paying customer.

Ch. 5: Digital Marketing on Social Networks

Over time, I've seen a lot of technophobes in the business world. Many of them assume that, since traditional marketing methods worked back in the day, then (obviously) they'll work again? And sometimes they're right. But, as stated previously, in marketing, the landscape is always changing. That's why we (as good marketers), must always be stoic—always accepting of this inevitable change.

Technology can be intimidating. But it is only through creative thinking that the most profitable marketing initiatives result. For decades, conventional advertising revolved around creating 90-second blurbs of content— typically for print, radio, and television. But that's not how we do things anymore. Modern online branding is different.

- Do you have a carpet cleaning company? If so, don't merely make a two-minute commercial about your service. Instead, create intriguing *how-to videos* that keep YouTube users engaged.
- Do you have a B2B company connecting clients to software? If so, don't just post news about software updates. Instead, start a Facebook discussion—asking users what they'd like to see from your app or what additional problems they wish it would solve.

In the 21st century, digital marketing is probably going to be your *tool of choice*—at least in the early days of your new startup.

- Millennials are far more likely to be influenced into making a purchase via personal blog posts and social media. In fact, they are 247% more likely to make buying decisions after perusing this type of content.
- It's also important to note that 93% of B2B sales are made after an initial online search was used by the consumer.
- Further, when polled, 7 out of 10 startups are actively using web content and social media for their inbound marketing strategies.

Now, if your startup is a local thrift shop or clothing store, conventional marketing may take precedence—at least initially. But even still, the world of digital marketing has a lot to offer conventional brick-and-mortar stores as well. In this chapter, we'll go through a few marketing fundamentals that apply to the digital domain.

The Benefits of Digital Marketing

There are many benefits to digital marketing. The primary one being that, when marketing in the online world is done correctly, it can be very effective—at an extremely affordable price. Even million-dollar companies can sometimes get away with spending nearly zero dollars on insanely successful advertising campaigns—if they manage to find the right brand face and following.

Digital marketing is unique because it often offers you a way to directly target your audience. In the days when the market was dominated by radio and television ads, advertisers could never really determine if their campaigns were working or not.

Traditional advertising is *disruptive*—meaning that your message only reaches an audience when they're busy consuming other media—like a soap opera or a ballgame. Digital marketing gives you a chance to connect with your audience—often at times when they're already engaged or in a favorable buying mindset. Additionally, most digital marketing channels provide resources and analytics for gauging campaign success—tools that were not available to traditional advertisers. Such tools grant advertisers with the freedom to adjust their marketing strategy as needed and to tailor it such that it is most effective in the given advertising channel. The benefits are clear. So let's break down the process a bit—so that you can see how it will work for your company.

Your Online Presence

There are over 7.8 billion people in the world and about 53.6% of them use the internet in some capacity. Around 3.8 billion of these users have social media accounts.

If you had a time machine and you could travel back to the 15th century, what is one invention that you could show people which would amaze them?

- Perhaps, in a time before electricity was put to use in cities, a simple light bulb would cause wonder?
- How about a photograph?
- A digital recording of a song or audio file?
- Maybe the ability to call someone on the other side of the planet?

Any one of these feats would be incredible. Fortunately for us, we can do them all with one device—our cellphones. We depend on our phones to provide us with communication and entertainment. But, more importantly for our purposes here, people now depend on their phones to buy things.

Out of all the traffic on the internet, 7 out of 10 bits are served up to a mobile device—a person using a cellphone or a tablet. And since 2019, 4 out of 5 emails are now opened via a mobile device instead of a PC.

So what does this mean for you?

- The first takeaway here is to understand the value of taking your marketing efforts to the digital domain. No matter how simple your website might be, an online presence is still essential.
- The second reminder is that your online presence has to be friendly to mobile devices. Note that mobile screens are much smaller than PC screens. Browsing conventional (non-responsive) websites can be tedious for mobile users. And, as their frustration builds up, customers leave your site and sales are lost. Let's take a moment to dive deeper into the value of maintaining a solid web presence.

Your Website

If you've already acquired a domain name and hosting services (i.e. if you already own a fully functional company website) then you might already be well on your way to digital success—give yourself a pat on the back (because most people never even get this far). But for the web newbies who haven't started their site yet, I thought I would throw in a few quick tips.

First, don't give anyone any money. If you go to Google and type in "how to build a website," then you'll be greeted with a cornucopia of possible web options— some offering very refined design services at very high prices. Generally speaking, this is not what you need for your new startup.

Unless your website must absolutely contain unique programming features, the cost of your initial website launch should be zero dollars. Additionally, do not attempt to teach yourself web design or coding. I'm a programmer and I can tell you, as a small business owner, it's usually not in your interest to dive into the world of web development—unless your business model revolves around selling custom web solutions or apps. Instead, just use a drag-and-drop website creator to get your company off the ground. And, once your online presence is established, you can always think about upgrading later.

In deciding which platform to host your website on, you basically have three major options these days:

1. A self-hosted site running WordPress
2. A SquareSpace site
3. A Wix.com site

If you're new to the online world, you want to go with Wix.com. Here, you can actually create a free website for "personal use," (you should consider upgrading to a "professional use" license once you become more established). Electing to go with this third option (Wix.com) is preferable because WordPress can be very challenging and intimidating for new web users. So start off easy and work your way up from there.

Creating Web Content

Recall in Chapter 2 when we described the difference between *inbound* and *outbound* marketing. To review:

- Outbound Marketing (interruption marketing) refers to traditional advertising methods which interrupt a consumer's regular viewing habits to show him a quick product message.
- Inbound Marketing is a technique to lure customers to your product pitch page by using

appealing content on your website, your social media channels, or on other web platforms.

When it comes to creating the pages of your company website, you can think of your site content as a giant inbound marketing lure. Many conventional online marketing books will insist that you have to "create a blog" in order to widen your online presence. But this is typically *not* the right way to craft a web content strategy.

Note that the word "blog" is a truncation of the words "web" and "log." And that's originally what blogs were meant to be— web logs. In other words, they are logs of a person's daily affairs—which have been placed on the web. Now, there is indeed a time and place to read the personal thoughts of another person's life. However, if you're trying to sell products to people on the internet, most of your inbound customers do not want to read a soliloquy about your dead cat before making a buying decision. This is the mistake that so many business owners make. Some entrepreneurs will attend a seminar or buy a book about "how to make money online" and some presenter will exclaim the virtues of blogging. Then the entrepreneur will go to the office and wax poetic about the daily affairs of their corporation. But most of them fail to realize that, for each post they make, it may have only been seen by two or three people. And, of the people who *did* see this blog post, most of them were *already* customers or fans to begin with—thus, they didn't need any more convincing. The point is, in the corporate world, most blogs are superfluous.

So don't treat your company website like a blog. Instead, treat it like a content lure. When your potential customers use Google, they are seeking a solution to their problems. They aren't going to be typing in queries about your cat. They'll be typing in things like:

- Why does my sink smell?
- How can I get stains out of my carpet?
- What's the best bed-and-breakfast hotel in Honolulu, Hawaii?
- What is the best laptop to buy this year?
- What can I wear with black socks?

The trick to creating marketable web content is not to create content about what *you* personally want to write about. Nor should be creating content about what *you* think your customers want to hear about. Instead, the trick is to create content that answers the questions that your customers are actually typing into Google.

One of the easiest ways to find this out, is to simply go to Google.com and start typing out phrases that relate to your product or service. For example, if you sell cameras, then try typing out partial queries like:

- What if my camera ____
- How do if fix my camera ____
- What's the best camera for ____

Notice that, as you type a little box appears below Google's search box. This is called the "list of autocomplete suggestions." Google creates this list based on the queries that real people are typing into their search engine. When a search phrase is entered into Google enough times, then it gets added to the list.

This can be a *very* valuable tool. Because, instead of just *guessing* about the type of content that we will be creating for our website, we can use the suggestions that appear in this box to mold our *content strategy* such that it reflects the searches that people are actually Googling.

For example, suppose you can see that people are Googling the phrase "How do I fix my **camera lens**?" Then, if you owned a camera website, this is perhaps the type of content that you are in a position to provide value for. People in the world are looking for tips and tricks that would reveal how or why their camera lens is not functioning. If you know how to answer this question, then one webpage on your company site could be devoted to teaching visitors how to examine their lens and determine the extent of the damage. Our goal in creating this page is not purely altruistic of course. Our goal is to get eyeballs on to our website. We want to provide valuable content. But on the bottom of our webpage, after the content is complete, we want to present a *call to action* (CTA). This call to action describes the method by which the user can take additional action on our website. This next action step might come in many different forms:

- Perhaps, at the bottom of your web article is a phone number—beckoning the visitor to call if he needs local camera lens repair services.

- Perhaps an email opt-in box appears on the bottom of the page—into which the user can type his email address and receive additional marketing material about camera lenses from your company.

- Or the CTA at the bottom may just be in the form of a series of links that lead to product pages on which you sell new lenses.

For new startups or small companies, there is no need to think of your web content development as a Hollywood movie studio would. It doesn't need any special effects or animations. You don't need to draw any highly technical images or hire expensive models. The important thing is just to offer good textual content and place attractive product photos at strategic locations along your website. Merely answering the user's question in a simple fashion and then giving him the choice to learn more about your product, can be a refreshingly simple technique for converting web visitors into buyers.

Social Media Marketing

The number of online social media users grows by the millions each year. Reportedly, social media is used by 9 out of 10 US millennials. (We think it's more like 10 out of 10; some of the millennials have got to be lying.) As the millennial generation ages (and as their children become ever more internet savvy), we can only assume that worldwide online media usage will continue to grow.

At one time, social media merely functioned as a way to exchange cat photos and chat about nothing. In 2007, Steve Jobs famously considered podcasting to be silly—calling it the "Wayne's World of the Internet." He was definitely wrong about that one. According to a study from the Interactive Advertising Bureau (IAB), podcasts are projected to generate $1 billion in revenue by the end of 2020.

Depending on your niche, social media can be an amazing way to amplify your business marketing efforts. Outputting the right piece of viral content can (potentially) make your company website explode overnight—brining in a torrent of world traffic. Never before in history have advertisers had access to so many tools with so much potential.

Choosing Your Social Media Channels

Generally, in life and business, you're better off focusing on one or two things; putting all of your effort into nurturing a relationship or a product, before moving on to construct more. The call to build *more* is a siren song—which every entrepreneur must struggle to ignore. As Steve Jobs said:

People think focus means saying "yes" to the thing you've got to focus on. But that's not what it means at all. It means saying "no" to the hundred other good ideas that there are. You have to pick carefully. I'm actually as proud of the things we haven't done as the things I have done. Innovation is saying "no" to 1,000 things.

Such advice is especially applicable to the world of social networking. There are over a million social media sites in the world, and there aren't enough hours in the day for you to maintain a presence on all of them. So don't try. In the early days of your startup, try to just stick with one or two networks. Develop your online presence there and familiarize yourself with the platform mechanics.

Below, we'll go over the top six social networks briefly:

1. Facebook has 2.6 billion active users. It's great for building and connecting with online communities. Most importantly, they have one of the biggest advertising networks on the web. And they're a demographer's dream—providing layer upon layer of juicy user data—allowing you to buy highly-targeted ads and track your results with the best analytics in the industry.

2. YouTube has 2 billion active users. Their platform is unique because, for the first time in history, business owners do not need to hire a film production crew and pay exorbitant network fees to present their product commercials to the world. Instead, YouTube allows you to stream all videos for free and these videos are instantly accessible all over the world—at zero cost to you. This means that you will always have a venue to get your product media out there. And if you can succeed in building a popular

YouTube following for your channel, then all the better.

3. Instagram has 1 billion active users. It's the new kid on the block but it's been growing quite virally over the last decade. Instagram influencers (people who own attractive Instagram accounts with many followers) are hired to pitch products or services. Recently, a lot of advertising dollars have flowed into this space. To get an idea of just how much, consider what the founder of Viral Nation Joe Gagliese told Vox, "A micro-influencer [someone that has 10,000 to 50,000 followers] is actually pretty valuable... They get a minimum of a few thousand dollars [per] post. Influencers with up to 1 million followers can get $10,000 [per post]... and [with] one million followers and up, you're getting into territory where they can charge $100,000 [per post]." As a new startup, you probably won't be spending a million dollars just on Instagram advertising. But, depending on your niche, it may be quite possible to attract new customers merely by pursuing some of the lesser-known Instagram influencers on the site—whose attention might be up for sale at a very reasonable price.

4. Twitter has 330 million active users. It's not the biggest social network, but it has a devoted fan base—each with their finger on the pulse of popular culture.

5. Pinterest has 320 million active users. Pinterest users tend to be female and the platform is obviously angled to provide a visual experience. It's a stunning contrast to the 140 character blurbs that one finds on Twitter. Most importantly, Pinterest gives each user a bottomless art board—on which they can forever post product photos. This makes it ideal for startups in the fashion or beauty niche. But also for any product that has a desirable exterior visual aesthetic.

6. LinkedIn has 260 million active users. And they're all about business. LinkedIn primarily functions as a platform for workers and employers to create business profiles and to foster professional relationships. So it can be great for nurturing your startup's presence in the business world. But LinkedIn also offers content hosting features—that allows professionals to post marketing videos or to create marketing content about their product or service.

Besides the top six social networks listed above, there are several others that shouldn't be looked over.

For example:

- Yelp
- Quora
- Reddit

- Tumblr
- Medium

Each of these platforms may indeed have a place in your social marketing campaign strategy. But remember, when you're first starting out, just pick one or two platforms to focus on.

Social Media Content Creation

There's a thin red line between a good piece of social media content and an *obnoxious* one. Unfortunately, many startups still manage to cross this line.

In the days of old, pushy sales techniques had some utility. Door-to-door salesmen would lug vacuum cleaners and encyclopedias onto each porch in the neighborhood, sometimes demanding that the homeowner buy something after the expense of such effort. In big department stores, perfume counter workers would lurk in doorways—waiting to aggressively approach wayward shoppers and spritz a new scent into their face. All while some other sales associate followed women into their dressing rooms— to try and force a sale while they were in their underwear.

These days, consumers want something more authentic. They don't want to feel pressured into buying something. Instead, they would like to feel like they are a part of something genuine and important. Social media is one of the tools we can use to manifest such emotions. This is why we must nurture our social media accounts slowly—rather than attempt to yank them up by the roots.

We all have that coworker, family member, or friend who seems to overshare on social media. From a fight with their partner to an unappetizing meal they're eating at Denny's, some people don't know when to hold back. The same can be said for certain brands.

Remember, in the world of social networks, we build communities. Meaning that, *interaction* is required for any community to grow. Though you may not be posting and creating content every single day, you (or your social media manager) can still check in on the platform—responding to messages and comments as needed.

Many young startups make the mistake of assuming that "more is better" in the online world. While it might seem like posting 3–5 times per day is a way to show off your brand and foster brand awareness, it can drive people away. As a general rule, it's typically best to post as much as you'd like to hear from a friend online. You don't need a string of constant updates, but checking in three times a week, or potentially daily, can be just the right amount. If your business happens to be in a particularly content-friendly niche—and you're creating funny, consumable, and highly-entertaining content, then do indeed post more. The content you share should be useful and have a purpose and a message. Can you teach your followers a little something more interesting than what they're used to seeing elsewhere? If you struggle to come up with creative ideas, don't be shy about holding off until inspiration strikes. Not every product is so readily shareable. Not every product photographs well—some services only exist as an idea or a text blurb.

Consider a résumé-building company for example. At first glance, this doesn't sound like the most social of companies to promote. There isn't much that's visually appealing about a page full of words—particularly when the page is about someone's work experience. However, there is actually a ton of room for creative social marketing with a business like this.

- You could post an article on "résumé tips" that employers are looking for.
- Share an infographic that describes why a certain résumé layout looks better than another.
- Offer a free downloadable résumé template file.
- Post a list of the ten most common interview questions that prospective hires should be prepared to answer.
- Or just share tips on "finding a job" in general.

The most important goal in your content-creation efforts is to make your content engaging. Ideally, we all want our content to be shared, "to go viral," and to (generally) just "spread the word" about our product or service.

Ch. 6: Old-School Marketing Strategies

Trends come in and out of our lives "like busboys in a restaurant." It's hard to be on social media for more than 20 minutes without seeing something that catches your eye—something unique, that you've never seen before. Even if you've filtered your search results to only provide you only with familiar information, social media will forever be a constant stream of new titillating media—ready to be absorbed by curious minds and hungry eyes. However, regardless of our newfound shift to the fast-paced online world, some old-school strategies still seem to work the best. The marketing fundamentals that worked over a century ago, can often still apply today.

Typically, even new tech companies will employ some

mix of both online and offline marketing (as well as inbound and outbound marketing). A cocktail of both is usually the best way to go. It is only after you have dipped your toes into both ponds that you get a sense of what the water is like in each one.

For startups, the main issue with off-line marketing is that it can initially be quite a bit more expensive—depending on the strategy employed. However, thanks to recent hybrids (between the offline and online worlds), traditional marketing has actually never been more affordable and easier to implement.

In advertising, we must always remain cognizant of the unique nature of each campaign. Raising companies is often like raising children. Even though they are sometimes quire similar, they often respond unpredictably to the same advertising strategy. Thus, there is often no *cookie cutter solution* that we can apply to all businesses. That's why we can't be afraid to think outside the box, and approach our marketing foibles with a stoic appreciation for the randomness of the universe.

Think of the last printed advertisement you received in the mail.

- Why did it grab your attention?
- What was it about the image that you found interesting?
- What aesthetic element caused you to want to buy the glossy product on its pages?

Attempting to identify that magic concoction of stimuli (which synergizes to convert a reader into a buyer) is our primary goal in the world of advertising. In this chapter, we'll go over some conventional techniques that have worked for marketers for generations.

Marketing via Print Material

Younger readers may be surprised to learn that the "end of paper" has been forecasted for a long time. Ever since computers started entering offices in the 60s and 70s, business people and futurists have heralded the arrival of the day when all paper media would be eliminated, and every piece of information would be accessible digitally.

Well, if you look around the landscape of the 21st century, you'll note that this prediction has still failed to come true. In fact, print and direct mail marketing ("junk mail" as it is often called) has never been more popular. Millions of consumers still purchase catalogs, journals, and newspapers. And astonishingly, a whopping 70% of drivers admit that billboards seem to have an effect on their purchasing decisions.

Though we live in the enlightened age of the digital domain, there is a lot to be said for getting a tangible piece of media into a potential customer's hands.

- Business cards
- Brochures
- Newspapers
- Leaflets
- Flyers
- Posters
- Stickers

Such articles are produced now more than ever. Why? Because they still work.

Creative stickers are often placed in public spaces. A gorgeous poster could be something that a person hangs in their apartment even if they don't know the brand very well. Such pieces of ephemera are capable of leaving a tactile impression—which is not possible in the online world.

When offering these printed materials, here are a few rules to stick to.

- First, we have already emphasized the importance of *brand consistency*. This rule (of course) applies to your printed material as well. The logo, font, colors, and the tone of the information you dispense, should coincide with all of your other pieces of branding media.

- Next, always ensure that your print media contains a tagline and a CTA (Call to Action). A tagline is a one-sentence blurb which tells the reader exactly what your company does—and how your company can make his life better. Your CTA should contain your company's contact information. But, more importantly, it should contain a reason for them to take action and get ahold of you. Don't be afraid to separate the "special business cards" from the "general business cards." Meaning that, there are some people in this world from whom your company would really benefit from—if you got a call back. For such people as this, you probably don't just want to give them the contact information of your secretary's landline. Instead, give them a card with your direct cellphone number on it. Or, better yet, write your cell phone number on the card with pen—so that this important person knows that you've just given him a direct line.

- Third, when giving out something like a brochure, try to make the exchange an informal proceeding. Thrusting media into another person's hands should not be an aggressive action. Instead, offer inquisitors with the potential to receive more knowledge about your product if the opportunity arises. The acceptance of a business card, a brochure, or a flyer is always a *possible* opener—to engage in more conversation with a potential client. But not an opportunity to attack him.

- Try to avoid waste. Eschew the urge to print out hundreds of flyers and stick them in between people's windshield wipers or mailboxes. Such guerilla marketing tactics have a place. And it is conceivable that this sort of strategy will work for some products or services. But, for most 21st century startup marketing efforts, we typically want to avoid such intrusive ventures. (Many of them are probably illegal in your town anyway.)

Product Unboxing, Packaging, and Loyalty Programs

Have you ever heard anyone say, "I just love their bags," or, "The jars this company uses look so cool!" For consumers, the *product packaging* and *unboxing* process is often the best part of the product-acquisition ritual. This is a curious phenomenon, which has only recently started to get attention—as evidenced by the thousands of "unboxing" channels on YouTube. People like to live through the experience of opening something new. This shouldn't be too surprising, since we all remember what Christmas morning was like.

Steve Jobs was (of course) a pro at this particular part of the product-creation process. Opening the spotless white box that houses your new iPhone or iMac is a magical experience—which has yet to be replicated in any other product I've seen.

This doesn't apply to all niches, but when appropriate, it is useful to think of your product packaging as (not something that will just be cast aside or thrown away), but instead, as something to be kept, admired, or used again by the customer. This usually means that the package design and materials will be more expensive. But, in a way, the construction of the package is actually a part of your marketing expense. Because, the package follows the customer home—it keeps doing the marketing work for you long after your sales staff has gone to bed.

Never underestimate the ability for "word of mouth" conversations to influence customers. It is the most powerful form of marketing there is. And if you can actually convince people to wear your brand on a t-shirt or hat, then you've just recruited an army of walking billboards.

Don't be afraid to give people things that are practical—even if they're unrelated to your business. Typically, companies will pass out key holders, toothbrushes, or water bottles at tradeshows and conventions. And that's fine. But ideally, you'll try to get a bit more creative with your tangible marketing items. Instead of a boring brochure, try putting your logo on an article that people will actually use—like a mousepad or a USB stick or an attractive refrigerator magnet. Remember, our goal is to create brand awareness— knowledge of our brand that will permeate the customer's field of view, if only for a transient moment. We can more aptly manifest this goal, if we can stick our logo on something the customer will actually use.

Television Spots

We can't put out a book on marketing without taking a moment to discuss one of the most prevalent of the traditional marketing channels—television. If you're a younger startup (particularly if you have a tech company), there's a good chance that television ads will not be of particular interest to you. However, take note that (as mentioned previously) all the major tech firms still use such conventional advertising channels. So, familiarizing yourself with all foundational techniques still has value.

Network television advertising is famous for launching a million brands while also being exceedingly expensive. If you have the budget to run a television ad on a major network show, then you're company is probably already on the right track—or, in the least, you've managed to convince some investors that it is.

However, many people don't realize how cheap it is to put out a commercial on a local television station. If your business services a regional clientele, local TV spots can be purchased for well under one-hundred dollars—often for quite a lot less. Most importantly, don't make the mistake of hiring a full production crew to make your commercials. These days, everyone carries a virtual editing station on their laptop. Film students and young movie creators would love to make your commercial for you—all at a price that is extremely modest. Often, such students have access to top-end equipment—which they borrow from the college they're attending.

So don't make the mistake of going to Google, searching for a production house near you, and calling the first high-priced production team that you stumble upon. Full-fledged production studios will try to sell you an entire brand experience and they use teams of well-paid professionals to create stunning media reels—but often at a very high price. When you're a new startup, this is often *not* what you're looking for. In fact, your first media spot often doesn't come out very good on the first try—no matter who you hire. If you'd like to see a great example of this, check out the first iPod commercial put out by Apple in 2001. It was horrible—merely featuring a guy in his lonely apartment—listening to music and awkwardly dancing. It wasn't until another year of trials and missteps that Apple landed on their iconic "dancing silhouette" advertising campaign—which is still mimicked to this day.

Making Connections

As most veteran business owners know, "networking" is often the most important marketing "trick" that a CEO can know. It is the *connections* that you make with other like-minded business owners or peers, which often lead to serendipitous encounters—resulting in moments of clarity or partnerships that lead to phenomenal business success. Typically, such rendezvous happen at:

- Conventions
- Trade shows
- Fairs
- Or other industry-related events

Such gatherings often function as just a pretense—luring like-minded people together with the promise of free pens and booth girls. All the while acknowledging that, *real connections* are typically not forged on the carpet of the convention center hall. Instead, they're made at the hotel bar or in the lobby.

Even so, your participation is at least required in the initial festivities. You can often buy a table at a convention or trade show on the cheap. And use this spot as a hub from which to network with other businesses.

Most importantly, when you're actively participating in such events, you'll have access to instant product feedback. You can hear what works and what doesn't—all directly from the mouths of consumers and competitors, just as they're standing in front of you.

Throughout our normal workdays, most of us are locked in a cubicle for the vast majority of the week. So, taking the time to encourage an actual tactile experience with a customer or competitor at such events is often quite eye opening.

Ch. 7: Marketing Without a Budget

Recall in Chapter three when we emphasized the importance of entering the marketing space with a marketing budget. In a sense, setting a hard line for your ad spend is like deciding how many "chips" you're willing to lose in the casino tonight. But, for young startups, your marketing budget may be very small or non-existent. If your company isn't bringing in much cash yet, what is a founder to do? In this chapter, we'll go over six tips that will enable you to spread the word about your venture, without spending too much money doing it.

Tip 1: Never underestimate the power of online product reviews

Nothing in life is truly free. What isn't spent in dollars is usually spent on time. Accordingly, it makes sense for consumers to peruse *product reviews* before making a product purchase. As online consumers, it is often the case that the only thing we have to go by is the (supposedly) "independent product reviews" that lie adjacent to each product photo. Curiously, about 9 out of 10 consumers state that the online reviews are "as trustworthy" as the recommendation they would receive from a friend. This behavior even carries over to the offline world. A similar proportion of consumers claim that they often "read reviews online" before visiting a brick-and-mortar business.

Such observations provide us with insight into the triggers that act as the primary lure for our products. You could own the fanciest restaurant in town—with thousands of dollars spent on daily marketing. But, if you get one bad review, your establishment might be no better off than the place across the street—which spent *no money* on marketing but has hundreds of positive reviews.

Product reviews are tricky for marketers—because we can't exactly pay for them the way that we pay for ad-space on a website. Instead. Our goal is to coax our customers into taking action and leaving a positive review on our *platform of choice*—be that Amazon.com, Google, or Yelp.

Ideally, whenever we have a happy customer, this customer will speak favorably about our product online. So, our job as marketers is to make the review-creation process as easy as possible. This is where most startup owners fail. When a customer expresses gratitude or remarks about the utility of the owner's product, he often merely replies with a "thank you." However, in the early days of a startup, this is a lost opportunity. Customers such as this should be encouraged to submit a genuine testimonial. To make this process as fluid as possible, many possible techniques could be employed.

- If you are running a brick-and-mortar establishment—like a restaurant or retail store, then you can prominently hang a poster up on the wall—which shows the customers exactly where and how to comment on your establishment. Often, eateries will do this for sites like Yelp. They may even keep a dedicated laptop behind the counter—on which customers can log-in and type a genuine positive review— right there at the bar.

- If your products are purchased via mail, then be sure to always include an information card in the package. This card will encourage the customer to go online and comment if he has a positive experience with the product. Importantly, on the same card, be sure to also include information about how the customer can *contact you* if he is having a bad experience with the product. You want to avoid a circumstance in which this customer takes to the internet—complaining about some failing of the product itself, instead of leaving a favorable review.

In one sentence, our primary goal here is to:

Make sure that all negative comments get to the owner and that all positive comments get to the internet.

If the reverse happens, that's when the trouble starts. In this newly connected age, you really don't want *any* negative comments to get to the internet (if possible). Avoid them like you would the plague, for they have been known to crush small businesses. (For an excellent report on this phenomena try Channel 4's "Attack of the Trip Advisors" in the UK.)

Tip 2: Give out Product Freebies to Influencers

What's the number one (tried and true) most timeless, classic, and dependable marketing strategy ever?

Word of mouth of course.

This is why *influencer marketing* is so popular right now— particularly on Instagram. We discussed the importance of hiring Instagram Influencers in previous chapters. But if you can't afford their fees right now, don't lose all hope. Almost every influencer has (at least at one time) accepted a free sample (a "product freebie") in exchange for a post, a tweet, or a link to your product webpage. The trick lies in finding an influencer who actually genuinely wants one of what you got, and then mailing your product to them. This is quite easy to do in some niches. For example, if you sell a *fashion product*, then you need only mail a few samples to a few up-and-coming Instagram accounts (ones that currently have lower follower metrics).

Such "baby Instagram accounts" love to get *free stuff*. And many will gladly tell their subscribers about the new "free gift they just got"—often without giving it a second thought nor demanding ancillary payment.

Be warned, however, that this doesn't always work. Some products are not very Instagram-friendly—like dishwasher soap or toilet bowl cleaner. So, before sending out thousands of dollars' worth of free product, try to make contact with the influencer and guarantee that your product is something that he or she will genuinely want to try out.

Tip 3: Join Online Communities

Previously, we talked about purchasing online ads and hiring online influencers. But what about posting your message in online communities?

Chances are, you started your startup company because you had a particular passion for a particular hobby. Indeed, there's a good chance that you were *already* generating content about similar products in an online social community before you even had the idea of creating a business about it.

- Did you have any influence in this community?
- Would members of this community buy your product if they knew about it?

Typically, the startup founder created a product that he knows will be useful to himself, as well as his friends. (This is how Apple computer was started of course. Steve Jobs and Steve Wozniak wanted a computer that they could use for their own personal hobbies.) On the internet, almost all online communities will tolerate some level of personal promotion. Meaning that, they allow members to casually promote their own goods and services, so long as the self-promotion doesn't intrude on the experience of the other members.

So, if you have some existing clout in an online community, then leverage it to your advantage. Try to befriend the community owner, and see if you can post some content that will lure community members over to your product or service webpage.

You don't have to limit your interactions to just one Facebook Group of course. Find as many like-minded communities as you can discover. Join them all. And follow the people who are the biggest influencers in the group. Make friends with the individuals at the top and do some networking. Often (particularly in the online world), such connections are the type of relationships that lead to the most effective organic marketing campaigns. And in turn, these campaigns can lead to extensive growth.

Tip 4: If you can't join a community, build a community

Aside from joining existing communities, you shouldn't be afraid to start *your own* community as well—possibly several of them. Remember, anyone can start a Facebook group for free. So consider starting one about a topic that runs parallel to the product you sell.

- If you sell children's storybooks, then start a Facebook group on parenting.
- If you sell classroom teaching aids, then start a Facebook group on elementary school education.
- If you sell vinyl stickers for automobiles, then start a Facebook group on sports cars.

Your goal is to create a group that offers actual content about these topics. But with the intent of casually interspersing links to your own product pages—ultimately with the goal of converting visitors into buyers. Typically, members understand that the owner of the Facebook group, often actually works in the industry that the group is about. So they are typically quite accepting of personal promotion from the

Facebook group owner—at least more so than from a random group member.

Any content you create in the group often has a multiplicative effect—because group members tend to share the content with other groups or friends. Funny memes, interesting facts, and pretty pictures often tend to generate clicks. And if you can intersperse such content with leads to your own product webpages, then all the better.

Tip 5: Give away your time and labor

Not only is it free to help others, but it's also a good thing to do in general. There's no denying that the world is filled with people in need. Have you ever seen one of those "sponsored by" signs?

- At the soup kitchen?
- On the side of the road?
- At the local Little League field?
- At the local community center?

It is quite common for local businesses to sponsor trash pickup or sporting events. Or even to take a day off work to bring the employees down to such events to "give back to the community." Of course, we all know that the reasoning behind such events is never purely altruistic. The sponsoring companies are getting free publicity. So take it when it comes. And don't be afraid to show your colors. If the outing requires participation from you (and multiple members of your staff), try giving your staff branded t-shirts—for your employees to wear while they're helping out. Try to incorporate clever techniques to get the community to connect with your brand and establish stronger bonds with those around you. If you have a product that (in some fashion) will be useful to the people you're helping, then try to give away as many as possible. Not all industries will benefit from local community outreach. But, particularly if you service a regional clientele, such events might be the best "free marketing" that can be mustered.

Tip 6: Publicize the founder's story

Have you ever watched a documentary on Steve Jobs or on Apple Computer? Have you ever seen a feel-good news story—about some local boy who has done well for himself? Why can't that story be about you?

If you're a young startup, then you might be thinking that no one will be interested in your story. Particularly, if you haven't hit the *million-dollar mark* yet. However, you might be surprised. Local reporters are always on the lookout for local companies who are starting new business models in the area. It's actually not very difficult to lure local reporters to your establishment if you have some sort of angle to the founding of your company.

- Is your startup company the source of some new type of technology?
- Are you a pioneer in your field?
- Does your product do something interesting?
- Do you have a "rags to riches" story?

You may be surprised to learn that both SpaceX founder Elon Musk and Amazon.com founder Jeff

Bezos both had local television stories done about their companies—long before either of them were nationally famous. (Some of these stores you can still watch on YouTube today.)

When you're sharing *your* story (whether it be in the local newspaper or online), you're providing reporters with a potentially interesting news article—and you're solving their problem (to find new content) for the day.

But if you can't lure any reporters over, don't be afraid to tell the story yourself—either via print or even via online video. The tale of the "local boy does well" is exactly the type of tale that people crave. If you manage to draw people in—such that they feel invested in *your* story—then they may want to look you up—and take further action to get to know who you are and what you're selling.

Ch. 8: Hiring a Marketing Company for your Startup

In the life of every entrepreneur, he or she is constantly making decisions about when to delegate and when to *not* delegate. This is a difficult question that should not be taken lightly. Hiring the wrong person can be a costly mistake. But *failing* to hire the right person can slow you down—forcing you to devote your attention to one aspect of your business at the expense of another.

Outsourcing (or delegating tasks) means you'll be able to free up some of your valuable time. Moments of your sentience can (instead) be devoted to the running of your business rather than on the management of individual components. Particularly when it comes to online marketing, there are a million tiny steps to learn—many of them quite technical in nature. And each has a tendency to stress out the most committed entrepreneur. You can't do it all:

- Are you going to learn how to do photo and video editing for your marketing ads or commercials?
- Do you know how to build a website and create engaging SEO-driven web content?
- Are you fast enough with a computer to setup and manage multiple social media accounts?

If you're not an expert in any of these fields now, then it may take you months to learn either one of these skills. So, your goal is to hire a freelancer, an agency, or an employee who can do these jobs better than you can.

Additionally, it can often be useful to depend on someone else for exterior product ideas. If you are the CEO of your own startup company, then there's a good chance you're also the "lead product creator." (E.g. you are the originator of your own product—as is particularly typical in the tech world.) If this is the case, it can often be difficult for the product creator to see his product from the customer's perspective. When you've worked with a product every day for so many years, then your brain may become blind to its flaws or to the way that others will perceive its marketability. To overcome this bias, it's usually helpful to rely on a second pair of eyes. So, in this chapter, we'll consider your options when it comes to hiring another set of eyes to help you on your way to marketing success.

How to Hire a Marketer

When it comes to hiring a marketer, we basically have two choices:

1. We can hire an independent freelancer—possibly taking on a new office employee.
2. Or, we can hire an marketing agency.

Let's consider each of these options now.

Option 1: Hiring Freelance Employees

Devising a marketing strategy requires the wearing of many different hats. To get your startup's campaign off the ground you're going to need:

- Pay-Per-Click (PPC) Campaign Managers
- Search Engine Optimization (SEO) Specialists
- Web Designers
- Web Server Administrators
- User Interface and User Experience Designers
- Social Media Managers
- Ad Buyers
- Video Creators
- Web Content Creators
- Photographers
- Copywriters
- Email Marketers
- And many more…

Given the complexities of the modern marketing space, it is rare (maybe impossible) to find a person who can do each of these tasks well. Consequently, most marketers tend to specialize on one or two items.

When your startup is young (and when your marketing budget is low), you'll have to consider a list of skills (like the above list) and attempt to determine which process will result in the greatest ROI (Return on Investment) for your marketing dollar. Unfortunately, nobody can answer this question for you—as it is entirely dependent upon the niche that your product happens to occupy.

Additionally, because of the persistent randomness of the marketing space, you will never know for sure if you have directed your marketing efforts into the right venue or not. So don't put all of your eggs in one basket. When your startup is young, play jazz. Don't be afraid to make lots of "little bets"—trying one technique for a month, then switching to another. This sort of vacillating behavior is ok when you're company is young and when you're still trying to develop a reservoir of knowledge—regarding which demographics will be most receptive to your product and which marketing techniques work the best.

This is why independent freelancers can be useful in the early days of a startup.

- Do you feel like Google Ads might be the best way to bring in new clients? Then hire a PPC guy to manage your AdWords campaign.
- Do you think you could benefit if you had a 90-second infomercial about your product available on YouTube or on your website homepage? Then hire a video creator to make one.
- Do you think that your company could benefit from a customer email list? Then hire a

copywriter to compose a series of influential emails.

Fortunately, such services can be purchased for very cheap on websites like Upwork (formerly Odesk), Freelancer.com, or even Fiverr.

Each time you work with a new freelancer, you'll learn a little bit more about how the world of marketing works. But, most importantly, you'll learn how receptive the world is (or is not) to your product or service. It's ok to approach your early marketing efforts as you would a buffet table. Since you're not really sure what combinations will taste the best, throw a little bit of everything on your plate. Just know when to "stop." Remember, we're only making *small bets* during our initial marketing efforts—often of amounts under one-thousand dollars per campaign.

So don't be afraid to work with several marketing service providers at first. And, once you've tried a few techniques (and you have developed a repository of reference experiences and marketing data points), then it will be time to sit back and evaluate which technique worked and which one didn't.

- Did your PPC advertising campaign bring in more money than it spent?
- Did people seem to like your 90-second commercial?
- Has your customer email list actually generated any sales?

The trick lies in sampling many advertising venues, sticking with the ones that work, and vacating the ones that fail.

Option 2: Hiring a Marketing Agency

Often in marketing, startup company fortunes are actually not built off of a chain of multiple successful marketing branches. Instead, the company's success is often derived from just one. Indeed, this one lucky break may have even happened via serendipity:

- That one Instagram Influencer who started wearing your headband every day—just because she loved it so much and sent thousands of life-long customers over to your webpage.
- That chance meeting with a celebrity during one drunken Christmas Party—which led to him promoting your product on Twitter for free.

- That artistic product image that you hired a student photographer to work on in Photoshop—which actually went viral and was spread around Pinterest—bringing you thousands of new customers for a year.

Such *chance events* often act as the accelerator that bootstraps a new startup into the realms of corporate success.

As your startup matures, so too will your marketing efforts. Eventually, one or two marketing strategies will shine through the others and will become the "go-to strategy" for your product—possibly for many years to come.

When this happens, it may be time to start moving away from freelancers, and to consider hiring a professional marketing agency. Alternatively, the opposite might be going on. It could be that your marketing efforts are stuck in a rut. Perhaps *none* of the things you've tried have managed to catch on. Maybe you've gone through several marketing freelancers with no success. Maybe you're tied down with other aspects of your business and you can't be bothered to spend any more time on marketing efforts at this junction. In such circumstances, this too might be the time to consider hiring a professional marketing agency.

Relationships with full-fledged marketing agencies often go best when you both have an idea of what you'd like to get out of the deal. Don't make the mistake of paying a million dollars for an artsy and ethereal 15-second commercial. Instead, when you approach a marketing company, you should be able to agree upon some *definition of success*. There are many possible data points that could be collected to quantify this request:

- If the marketing agency is creating a commercial for you, then be sure that this video has a unique phone number on it (as opposed to your regular office number). That way, you can track the number of calls that this commercial generates.
- If the marketing agency is creating a series of conventional mailers for you, then make sure that the contact information on these mailers is unique as well—so you can track the responses from each series.
- If the marketing agency is creating a web form for your website, then be sure to contrast their web data with that of your existing data. So you

can know if the performance of the new form has managed to convert more visitors into subscribers than the previous web form.

By agreeing upon a *definition of success* early in the negotiation process, you are letting the marketing company know exactly what you expect of them.

Remember, as we've tried to emphasize many times in this book, marketing is about *trial and error*. By fastidiously logging these errors, we track and build ever-increasing awareness about the utility of each marketing effort. It is only via this accumulation of knowledge (particularly about things that do *not* work), that we can develop a better understanding of the things that *do* work.

Whether you decide to work with a freelancer or a marketing agency, the rules are the same. Evaluate the resultant data from each campaign when it becomes available. Then, consider the state of your company at that point in time—and make *course corrections* when necessary.

Don't try to rush the process. Successful marketing often evolves via a series of cautious steps. You can't actually skip any given step and arrive at a winning solution in one leap. Instead, each step must be hard-won. Each step must be laboriously traversed. But, when you arrive at the *top step*, you should find yourself sitting on a very sturdy foundation for success.

Finding Your Marketing Partner

When it comes to deciding who you're going to work with, there is a common set of principles that one might request from both agencies and freelancers. There are many experts out there to choose from. Finding a marketing partner who jives with your startup culture and is in-tune with your own corporate goals, can be a tedious undertaking. Some marketing pairings are just not meant to be. The type of marketer that would be best for a local brick-and-mortar business (selling some mundane product or service via snail mail), would often not be the same marketer that would fit well with a new mobile app company.

Often, the best way to tell if a marketer is going to be a good fit for *your* company is to simply request a list of all the *other* companies that he has worked with in the past. If the products of the companies on this list seem to be congruous with that of your own, then there's a good chance that you may have found the right man for the job.

Either way, communication is key. And it's important to outline the type of interaction that you will be engaging in during the marketing campaigns. Take time to consider the communication process of the marketing company before you hire them. Personality types come into play here. Some entrepreneurs insist on micromanaging every employee and overseeing every project. While others are very *hands-off*. So, discuss the modes of interaction upfront:

- Are you going to be working one-on-one with this marketer?

- Will it be an *online-only* effort, or will you be meeting in-person?
- *Where* will you be meeting? In his office or yours?

I suggest avoiding the "online-only" approach. If you plan on being in business for a while, you'll eventually have to build a relationship with the marketer who is responsible for your case. By hiring a local company (preferably one that's less than twenty minutes from your office), you facilitate the relationship-building process. By taking the time for face-to-face encounters, both parties can manifest the transmission of those ineffable subtleties of discourse—which are so important in the construction of long-term trust. And, when it comes to marketing, *trust* is everything.

Conclusion

Typically, when an entrepreneur first stumbles upon his initial startup idea, his mind races through a series of infinite possibilities. This can be a special time for a new company. A time of hope and fear. A time of optimism—about a future of success and maybe even an opportunity to make the world a better place. That first flutter of hope is a powerful one. And it is often the very force that has led you to seek out this book.

But, behind the misty clouds of that lofty excitement, lies a great mountain to climb. A mountain of work; lots of work. The 80+ hours per week that will be required of an entrepreneur to get his business off the ground.

As business owners, we are the conductors of a great orchestra. But we often start out as violin players. Eventually, we all learn that we can't play every instrument ourselves. We only have two hands. So we hire people. We outsource. We take on ancillary agencies to help us grow our business. When done correctly, such moves can amplify your efforts—turning your two hands into fifty. But when done incorrectly, you might find yourself leading a grand cacophony of out-of-sync musicians—each one failing to play the notes needed to bring about your symphony arrangement.

When such failings happen, that original glimmer of hope can become a forest fire of destruction. Our startup entrepreneur may start to despise his own company and the amount of attention it demands of him.

Michael Gerber has written about this phenomenon for decades. In his book *"The E-Myth Revisited: Why Most Small Businesses Don't Work and What to Do About It"* Gerber tells the tales of many business owners who were so overwhelmed by the demands of their own companies that they would often be in tears at the end of each workday. Why? Because they are a victim of the "e-myth." This is the myth that small businesses are started by entrepreneurs who hope to turn investment capital into profit. But in actuality, new businesses are usually started by hobbyists—hoping to make a little money out of their craft.

Because the initial mindset that goes into founding a startup is so often not conducive to the flow of daily business operations, the founder can often get perplexed, frustrated, and decide to *close up shop* entirely.

The solution to this conundrum is to think of your business as a *system* not as a hobby. Gerber writes:

> **The system runs the business. The people run the system. In the Franchise Prototype, the system becomes the solution to the problems that have beset all businesses, and all human organizations since time immemorial. The system integrates all the elements required to make a business work. It transforms a business into a machine, or more accurately, because it is so alive, into an organism, driven by the integrity of its parts, all working in concert toward a realized objective.**

Hiring a marketing agency or a freelancer is no different than hiring any other employee. Your goal is to find someone who knows how to play the *song of your company*. When you find a marketer who knows how to strike the right notes for your brand, then the harmony that emanates from such a partnership can be sublime.

If there's one thing to remember throughout the startup-founding process, it's that the entire affair is indeed a process. Successful businesses are not just quick productions—comprised of easy feats and tawdry tales. Instead, they are grand representations of the ideals of their founders (and often the children of these founders.)

When you inevitably encounter setbacks, don't react with anger or rage. Being an entrepreneur means accepting *change* and committing to a lifestyle that welcomes the peaks and valleys on which the rollercoasters of the business world ride. Always strive to remain cognizant of the fact that:

- Most of the products that have ever been created, have failed.

- Most of the marketing campaigns that have ever been executed, have failed.

The Pareto principle dictates that 80% of the positive results of your business efforts will come from just 20% of your actions. Meaning that, if you work ten hours each day, then eight of those hours are of relatively little value. If you're not familiar with this concept, you should take a moment to reflect upon that—and come back to it again (and again) in the future. It can be a humbling fact to fully absorb.

As entrepreneurs, we like to think we're always "working hard." But, just be aware that most of your actions have little value to your business success in aggregate. This is the nature of the beast. We have to learn to accept the randomness of the universe as "just a part of the job." So don't get too absorbed in ruminating over any single business failure, product failure, or marketing failure.

Instead, focus on learning from each mistake, and on reducing the probability of making the same mistake in the future. Such is the nature of the actual path to momentous marketing success. I wish you luck on your journey.

Printed in Great Britain
by Amazon